I0441594

# Copyright

The Safari in Africa Serengeti Families is a fictional book. The story is based on the annual great migration in the Serengeti National Park in Africa. The characters and incidents in the story are the product of the author's imagination.

Copyright © 2011 by Snow White
All rights reserved. Except as permitted under the U.S. Copyright Act of 1976, no part of this publication maybe reproduced, distributed, or transmitted in any form or by any means, or stored in a database or retrieval system, without the prior written permission of the publisher.

To all wildlife conservationists whose hard work preserved
a piece of nature's beauty and wonder!

# Contents

# Introduction

Welcome to the Serengeti and the Maasai Mara plains! In this area, the awesome spectacle of two millions of wildebeest, zebra and Tomson's gazelle stampeding their annual-migration route for two millions of years has made itself the seventh New Wonder of the World. This spectacular land animal movement is found nowhere else on earth but in the Serengeti. What prompts this massive exodus in the animal kingdom? How do they do it? What impacts have resulted from it? We will find out in this book about the Serengeti and Serengeti families.

In the Maasai language the word Serengeti means an "extended plain". Indeed, the place covers 15,500 square miles of grassland, straddling two African countries, Kenya and Tanzania. It is an area teemed with wildlife. At its heart is the Serengeti National Park. It's one of the best-known wildlife sanctuaries in the world, and symbolizes the classic African safari.

Modern scientists who study human origins through DNA research or archeological findings believe the human story begins in Africa. In other words, a visit to the Serengeti is like a journey back to an earlier time—the Stone Age. We can draw a parallel between today's wild animals and early Homo sapiens living in caves. Cavemen, like all other animals, depended on what ever nature provided for their survival.

Later on Homo sapiens evolved into a very successful species, and had dominion over other species. But humans didn't emerge as conquerors without paying big-time. As a matter of fact, humans suffered as much as wild animals in terms of being inflicted with diseases and natural disasters for a long time. Only since industrial revolution have modern men started to enjoy the fruits of civilization. We as humans, nowadays, should be sensitive enough to animals' welfare, for with whom we shared an ancient past. We were in their shoes not too long ago.

All species are driven by one primitive instinct: how to survive. Who gets to survive? The rule of the jungle: *survival of the fittest*. Darwin meant the phrase as a metaphor for better adapted for immediate, local environment, not the common inference of in the best physical shape. However, what we see in the jungle or in the wild the survival belongs no less to the most adaptable than to the strongest (in the best physical shape). In short, you are either eating or eaten in the wild.

For two million years, every year a mega-herd of wildebeest, zebra and Tomson's gazelle completes its annual migration, a 650 miles circle in search of fresh pastures for new grass to graze. This is a journey with danger lurking at every twist and turn. One quarter of them will be killed by predators, diseases and drowning. Yet they are running, unstoppable; they must do it because the alternative is starvation.

It started with a natural phenomenon, that phenomenon fed another phenomenon…and so on. The Serengeti is what it is—rich soil and endless open plain—results from the volcanic ash that spilled out millions of years ago. The savannah is dotted with volcanoes: Ngorongoro, Mount Kenya, Mount Kilimanjaro and Olenguruon, etc. Over millions of years the rains turned the ash-covered plains into hard-cement-like deposit, impenetrable to plants with deep roots. Gradually, the upper layer of ash turned into soft soil, loaded with nutrients and idea for grasses. Without the invasion of deep-rooted trees, the grasses thrive, outstretching into an undulating green sea. Here, flora and fauna grow and multiply. Here, a volcanic legacy kicked off and sustained the largest land migration in the world.

Mega-herd's running for lifeline benefits many predators, allowing their species to prosper. Feeding on the herbivores, the predators thin out the herd to avoid overpopulation and overgrazing. Mega-herd's dung fertilizes the soil and its saliva stimulates the grass to grow. The whole scheme of organisms and non-organisms interacting together is called the ecosystem. When the ecosystem is broken or unbalanced, the alternative can be devastating.

The great migration in the Serengeti is brought about on one hand by natural phenomena such as endless plains, rich soil, and synchronized rainy seasons, on the other the struggle for survival on the part of the animals. Doesn't the human history tell the same story in a more complex fashion? Don't we see every culture has a similar story like the Israelites' Exodus from Egypt?

Family is the basic unit in human-survival scheme. Animals, too, form family units in their survival design. Like human family, in animal family the mother is the one with the responsibility of rearing the young. A strong mother usually brings up most of her young to maturity. A weak mother can loose all of them. A species that has a lot of successful families is a prosperous species. Life is literally a constant struggle for the families in the wild, especially for the mothers. We can easily find animal family sagas with ups and downs no less interesting than humans'.

## The Exodus

Meet Moses, the stallion in the zebra herd, who is checking the grazing patch of his harem. He wants to know whether the patch has enough grass for all to feed, or not. He is troubled when he sees not too many tall grasses are left for the family to feed on. He trots away to scout for a better patch. He finally finds one after jumping several muddy bogs and skipping some barren patches. He leads his family of four ladies to the new patch. They are all exhilarated.

*"Good job, one patch with edible grasses. Thank you! Moses,"* says Ruth, the leader of the mares, *"isn't it about time for the mega-herd to move south for new pastures? See, here in Maasai-Mara, grasses are pretty much all cleaned up. The relentless rains have torn the ground into a muddy mess. I hate to walk on this sticky, muddy ground."*

Moses is a male, Burchell zebra. He stands five feet tall at the shoulder, weighs five hundred fifty pounds. His long legs, large ears, and massive head, muscular body make him look very handsome. His shining coat imprinted with black and white stripes not only embellishes his image, but also serves the purpose of withstanding solar radiation and providing camouflage.

Zebra form family groups called *harems.* A harem can have two to five mares (females) and is led by a stallion, living in a long-term, family-like relationship. The mares may have foals. Each foal follows its own mother. Family members stand together and nibble the hair on each other's neck and back. This grooming builds family bond. They look out for one another. Should one become separated from the rest, the others would search for it. Sharp-eye zebra are always on the lookout for sneaking hunters. When one zebra spots a suspicious predator, he immediately sounds alarm call that ripples through the herds. When on the road, the group adjusts its traveling pace to accommodate the old and the weak.

The females observe a hierarchical order when marching. A dominant mare leads the group, followed by the second in rank, and so on in a single file, each with their foals right behind them.

The stallion defends his females from rival males and predators. Like a commander he leads the way, strategizing when faced with road blocks. He doesn't play a role in the mares' single file. He gallops up and down outside the line. When necessary he stays behind, ready to kick any intruder who's on their tails. He keeps a close eye on the mega-herd's movement, listening for alarms.

*"Well, Ruth,"* replies Moses with a firm voice, *"any day I promise. We are waiting for the clouds, and the clouds should appear any day soon."* In Moses' calculation, every year around this time the sky to the south is covered with dark clouds, signaling the start of rainy seasons. Just in time for the mega-herd of two million herbivores to depart from their current location Maasai-Mara where food is becoming meager to a new land of bounty.

\*\*\*\*\*\*\*\*\*\*\*\*\*\*\*\*\*\*

A few days later, just as Moses expected, the sky to the south is covered with dark clouds. You can even hear roaring thunder in a distance. Excited he summons his group to step into a single file and march south down the horizon. During the time that Moses is galloping up and down to get his harem in line, the other zebra groups are also kicked into gear. Like a domino effect the momentum catches on from zebra to wildebeest and to Tomson's gazelle.

It is November. One sees a mass of 1.2 million wildebeest, 500, 000 Tomson's gazelle, and 300,000 zebra congregate in the north point of its annual route in Maasai-Mara, ready to march to a new terrain. The sheer numbers make this congregation the highest density of animal groups on earth, an awesome view acclaimed as the seventh New Wonder of the World.

To move a mass of this magnitude, one can't help asking: How does the mass of the mega-herd stick together? How do they keep order? What do they do not to get lost? How do they set the course?

For zebra it is easy. Zebra live in a strict, social structure. Zebra herd is composed of groups of harems. Each harem is led by a stallion, assisted by a dominant mare. Members follow the leaders. Compared to zebra, wildebeest and gazelle are socially inept. There is no unity in their midst. They only have loosely formed groups during mating season. Simple society has a simple rule: stay next to another of your own kind. One wildebeest will follow another wildebeest. One gazelle will follow another gazelle. For the foals, it is critical for them to stick to their mothers. The ones who do not stay with their mothers surly die.

How do they set the course? They don't have a set course to repeat year after year. They follow the rains. Because where it rains the fresh grass follows. They let themselves be guided by the signs in the sky: clouds, thunder and lightening. Since the rains are subject to climate change, the migration itinerary changes every year, too.

The journey is clockwise around the Serengeti, but it is not a straight, simple loop. The herds may split and regroup at various points, either enticed by the green pasture or forced by spooky danger. Overall the marching troop maintains its visibility clockwise around the Serengeti.

The Serengeti mega-herd makes a dramatic exodus from the muddy Maasai-Mara. Three distinct columns of wildebeest, gazelle and zebra strung out, each up to 25 miles long, are stampeding towards the rain clouds to the south horizon. The migration is on the move through Loliondo and the east side of the Serengeti National Park. Out of the three columns zebra leads in front. Zebra will arrive first and browse before wildebeest do.

*"Ladies, the green carpet is in sight. Can we accelerate our speed? We are almost there. We've got to beat the wildebeest and arrive first. You know how clumsy the wildebeest are. They trample the grasses with oblivion while they eat,"* says Moses in order to spur

his group into high gear. Moses feels the group could run faster, and he is nervous that the other zebra groups are passing them by.

*"Moses, I am afraid this is the fastest I can run. As a matter of fact, I need to slow down. You know I am nine months pregnant. I am hungry and I am tired,"* complains Hagar. Hagar is the youngest of the mares in the harem. She is the only one who is pregnant; the others had their foals a few years ago. Now their young are grown and stay in a bachelor group.

*"I'm sorry, Hagar, I should've been more thoughtful about your physical condition. We can adjust to your traveling pace,"* apologies Moses. Given his strong will, Moses can be pushy. But he has a soft side as well. He is especially soft with the weak and old.

\*\*\*\*\*\*\*\*\*\*\*\*\*\*\*\*\*\*\*\*\*\*\*\*\*\*

Rebecca, a female wildebeest, is also on the move lolloping. Her strange rocking gallop, even though it doesn't look elegant, saves her energy and keeps her momentum. She is six months pregnant, and this is her fourth pregnancy. She feels fortunate that she was able to raise two out of three her calves to adulthood. The first one she lost it to a crocodile when crossing the Grumeti River. The other two are fully grown. Something she is so proud of.

Motherhood in wildebeest herd is tough because there is no support system in the herd. Every mother is for herself. No nursing female will allow suckling other than her own calf. They will even show hostility towards other calves as approached. God help the young that has gotten lost!

Wildebeest are funny-looking animals—a walking conundrum. Our Creator must have assembled them out of spare parts of other species. The forequarter comes from an ox, the hindquarter is taken from an antelope, and the mane and tail are from a horse. When put together, you have a disproportionate body with the front end heavily built, the hindquarters slim. They are grayish brown with black vertical stripes. Both males and females have curving horns.

10

They are marathon runners with stamina and endurance. They can run as fast as the zebra, but they lag behind the zebra for lack of discipline and social structure. There is no formation of groups for a long-term relationship. Only during mating season, breeding groups of about 100 animals are formed. In these small groups, strong bulls will engage in combat several times a day, fighting with their horns to establish dominance and the boundaries of their territories. In this way, the accepted boundaries of the territory can change on a daily basis. As the female groups pass through, the territorial males will try to herd them to prevent them from leaving. The make-up of the group members can change by the hour. There can be no long-term relationship existed with the couple.

So far, Rebecca has done quite well in rearing her children. Single-handedly, she nursed them, taught them and protected them. Her secret of success is: be alert and stick to the herd. And that's what she passes on to her children. She hopes this calving season, her baby will be born safely in the midst of wildebeest herd.

\*\*\*\*\*\*\*\*\*\*\*\*\*\*\*\*\*\*\*\*\*\*\*\*\*\*\*\*\*\*\*\*\*\*\*

Edith, a female Tomson's gazelle, is pregnant too. She is three months pregnant and her due is in three months. That is because gazelle's gestation period is six months. She has light brown coat with white belly. A distinctive black stripe divides the topside coat and underside belly. There is a white patch on her rump. Her tail is vacillating in constant motion. Her spindly legs bounce like a ballet dancer. Unlike the male, she has no horns.

A noticeable tribute of Thomson's gazelles is their bounding leap, known as stotting or pronking, used to display strength and deter predators. They leap around before an attack, as if saying, *"I'm too nimble for you, so don't even bother."* Their top speed is seventy miles per hour. When spooked, their tiny bodies can just fly in mid-air. Given their speed and agility, most the time they outrun their hunters.

Like the wildebeest, Tomson's gazelle have no strict, social structure. Only during mating season do they form groups: territorial-male groups and female groups. Adult males buck around in their territories will clash their horns with rivals. Their mating right comes with the establishment of the territory. Like the wildebeest, a gazelle has no long-term relationship with its mate.

Edith has given birth eight times. Single foal at each birth. Out of eight foals only three made out alive. The other five were eaten by cheetahs and hyenas. The foals are easy targets for the carnivores. Due to the birth struggle, both the mother and the newborn are physically weak and slow in response. They fall easy prey to the predators. Edith hopes this time she will have a safe delivery, escaping the deadly claws of predators.

***************

As soon as the mega-herd arrives on the east side of the short-grass plains, the rains fall. The dry season is over. Much needed rain is at hand. Quickly the parched plains soak it all up. New grass begins to sprout. Within a few days, the eastern Serengeti is covered with nutritious green grass for the herbivores. The animals are delighted to see a carpet of food at their hooves. This is, indeed, the promised land, a land of bounty for these animals. The succulent grass is what makes all the stampeding and chasing worth all the efforts and risk.

There, the herbivores are grazing in harmony. No fights. Why aren't they fighting for the grass? The reason is simple: they don't eat the same plants. The zebra browse the shrub, the tall grass. The wildebeest prefer the short grass. Their wide mouths crop the grass down to the base and often miss out some spots. The gazelle comes in nibbling up the shoots missed by the wildebeest. This eating arrangement allows the food sources to be divided harmoniously to each one's delight. As a result, three very distinct species, total two million animals can live side by side year round without conflict.

Now they are in the first phase of the migration odyssey. From November to February they are marching around in the Serengeti eastern corridor. In the second phase in March when short-grass plains are starting to take strain, the stampeding hooves will be moving through woodlands towards the western corridor and back to Kenya.

Paradoxically, their lifeline route is concealed with threats and danger. On the eastern-corridor-open grasslands, there are less covers for leopards, lions and baboons; thus there are less of them. However, hyenas and cheetahs, who don't rely on as much cover, are numerous and devastating to the mega-herd. In the western corridor and north where woodlands are outspread, rocks and trees are home to lions and leopards. The situation is dicey. What's more? The rough terrains force the herds to split into small groups and go their separate routes. Their pathways are spooky and perilous. If that weren't enough, they have to cross two rivers infested with Nile crocodiles.

# Cheetah Mom Trains Her Cubs

Eve, a female cheetah, is scanning on the top of a termite mount for potential prey. Outstretching from her eye level is an endless-open plain, of which the color is gradually turning from brown to green. With her strong animal senses she is expecting the familiar scene of a mass of hooves and horns dotting the open plain at any day. Every year after a long dry season the rain would come. That signifies the abundance of food supply to her and her three cubs. She is glad because now the cubs are old enough to learn how to hunt. They need some hands-on practice. The return of the mega-herd will provide just that.

The three cubs are two males and one female. They are a loving family. The cubs love nothing better than hanging around their mom: swatting her tail, turning somersaults on mom's back, and cuddling underneath her belly. Their playfulness sends them to chase each other across the plain, up and down hills or up and down trees. Their favorite game is ambushing one another. At the most exciting moment of the onslaught you have one big pile of heads, paws and tails. The rough-and-tumble prepares them for the hunting skills that they need later on.

Eve's mate, the father of the cubs, is rarely seen. After the birth of the cubs, he spared himself from being a nuisance and wandered off. He doesn't play a permanent role in our cheetah family's growing up together. He does, occasionally, drop in to visit the family in a distance and drops off a prize for the family to feed on.

Eve spots a single file of warthogs trotting across the plain. She leaps off the termite mount into the field. Her narrow, streamline body zips through, sixty-five miles per hour. In a second she is right behind the piglet. Effortlessly she picks up the piglet and speeds away with the piglet dangling in her mouth. The screaming of the piglet causes the warthog mother to chase after the cheetah. But it is too late. The mother knows that her child will be killed in a second.

Seeing their mom bring a kill home, the cubs make merry. Last time the boys got to open the carcass; this time the girl wants to do it. She pushes her two brothers off and jumps on the soft part of the belly, starting to tear into the skin. These cubs are one year old. Less than a year they should have perfected their hunting skills and should be able to live independently. They are now where they should be. That is, their hunting techniques amount to nothing more than game play.

Quickly and quietly, the family gobbles down the carcass. In the open plain they are easily spotted by other predators like vultures, hyenas and lions. Those predators want their shares of carcass, even though they didn't take part in the hunt. That is called scavenging. Cheetahs, being the lightest in weight among the carnivores, offer no resistance when their hard-earned prize is stolen. The only way to assert their right on the carcass is to eat it quickly before anybody else finds out about it.

In the evening, the family huddles together grooming, using each other's back as a couch to recline on…their legs outstretched and relaxed. All of a sudden, mom jumps up. Not too far, a lioness is walking towards them. Lions cannot tolerate another predator in their territories. Cubs are to be eliminated. One less cheetah cub means one less adult cheetah in the future.

Mother instinct kicks in. Eve stands up, making herself look big and tall, and rallies her muscles, summons her courage to fight the queen of the beasts. She must know that she stands no chance in the fight. The lioness is twice her size, twice her weight. But she is driven by her love for her children. She loves her children so much that she is going to lay down her life to protect them from the lioness.

Part of the cheetah's territory overlaps with a lion den. More often than not lions pass through her turf. Since lions are on the top of the food chain, they have no qualms in roaming through the cheetah's backyard. But the cheetahs would all tense up and would immediately switch into a fight-or-flight mode. Our cheetah mom lost her young cub to a roaming lioness when she was away scouring for food six months ago. She is not to let that happen again.

Bravely, Eve moves towards the lioness, trying to divert her away from her cubs. She growls at the lioness with anger and determination. The lioness takes a step back. *"Wow, this cheetah is mad. Doesn't she know I can wipe her out just like that? Is she sick?"* She is surprised by cheetah mom's aggression. In her bewildering she makes a detour and runs away when Eve charges her.

******************

The day has come. Down the horizon, a cloud of dust heralds the arrival of the stampeding mega-herd. Eve's anxious eyes stare at it. Her heart is pumping fast. *"Hurrah! Here comes the feast that we've been waiting for."* Just the thought of it makes her mouth drool. She does her little dance to welcome the season. The cubs, seeing mom so perked up, join in to have their share of fun.

In a few days the herbivores have scattered all over the plains. Their presence attracts as much attention from our cheetah family as from lions and hyenas. Each predator hones its unique hunting techniques. Lions are sprinters with the burst of energy that gives them a flying start; they ambush and wrestle down prey with their mighty power. Hyenas are marathon runners with stamina and endurance; they skip stalking and chase prey directly up to three miles long. Both are formidable group hunters. All have families to feed. Our cheetah mom has tough competitors to deal with. Her talent is her speed; her top speed is seventy-five miles per hour. Being the fastest land animal, she's got an edge.

Cheetahs possess a number of vocalizations: chirping, stuttering, growling, yowling, and purring. When Eve calls to her children, she chirps. The cubs chirp back like little birds. This is how they make contact with each other. To warn about danger Eve yowls. Like now, she sees a buffalo moseying not too far away. She wants to tell her cubs this is a dangerous animal, keep off. She yowls, which is a low-gurgling sound. The cubs stay still, close to mom and learn not to chase the buffalo.

16

As part of preparation for hunting, Eve scans the landscape from the top of the termite mount. From there she has a panoramic view of the savannah that is teemed with wildlife. This tapestry comes to life with running, grunting animals. Nothing escapes her keen eyes. In a cloud of dust a wildebeest is struggling for life; a pack of hyenas is on top of him. In another corner, a group of lions is chasing a zebra. As for herself, she is looking for a young gazelle to bring home to her cubs for practice.

Not only is Eve an excellent hunter, she is also a good teacher. To pass on that legacy, she will introduce step-by-step lessons to her cubs. Having an understanding of how crucial it is for her cubs to make a connection between *play* with prey like a toy and *hunt and kill* for food, she'll need a live prey.

*"There is a young gazelle, drifting away from its mother, a perfect target. Boys and girl, let's go get it!"* Excited, the whole family jumps into action. Whereas the mother bolts into the field like a shooting bullet, the cubs are lagging way behind, trying to catch up with mom.

Her light-framed body whips through wind; her movement is as supple as silk. When the gap is narrowed, Eve skids to a stop and takes cover in the tall grass. She lowers her body into position, slinking forward. She was downwind of the young gazelle, so he is unaware of being stalked. In a flash, Eve springs out of the grass and chases. The highly alert young gazelle senses a sinister force hurled at him, and picks up his legs, running for his life. He can feel the cheetah's incredible speed and power. To escape he makes a sharp turn, hoping to lose his chaser. Eve, being an experienced hunter, extends her dewclaw and trips the young gazelle's hind leg. The young gazelle tumbles on the ground. Eve scoops him up in her mouth, being careful enough not to kill the young gazelle.

After the burst of the high speed chase, Eve stops and pants to catch oxygen. While she is huffing and puffing, her cubs are scampering into the scene to meet the young animal.

*"I cannot believe mom has brought us a live prey. What are we supposed to do with it?"* asks the girl with a puzzled look on her innocent face. She just shed her baby hair not long ago.

*"We are to eat it. This time we get to open the carcass,"* reply the boys.

*"No, no! Boys and girl, you got to kill it before you can eat it. Today is a special day, a day you get to put your training into practice. Now, I am to release the prey and let you chase. Remember to trip its hind leg,"* Eve admonishes the cubs and turns loose the young gazelle. Thus a new frontier opens up in their training session.

The fawn is scared to death. He freezes and remains still. The prey isn't running; the cubs don't know what to do. They know to chase a moving target; they don't know what to do with a fixed object. After a few seconds of standoff, the fawn bounds off. The chase is on.

The three cubs are on the fawn's tail chasing. The big brother is the fastest runner. He trips the fawn's hind leg just like what he saw mom did. *Plop!* The fawn drops to the ground. The cubs' adrenalines shoot up, the killing instinct kicks in. Something triggers inside, these cubs are becoming hunters. The cubs jump on the victim's throat and execute "the kill". Seeing the victim is still struggling because the cubs' bites are shallow, Eve moves in and finishes the job. They have marked their milestone; the cubs have learned to chase, to trip and kill. Mom is happy with her children's resounding success.

## The Casualty

After a day's grass munching, the mega-herd rests at night. Their night vision is poor. In the dark they probably can only make out a silhouette of their enemy. This is the time the lookout system, watching out for one another, will be tested to the zenith.

The zebra, being the most sociable, in order to look after one another are vigilant like being wired to an alarm system. The other species, wildebeest and gazelle, will respond to zebra's alarm call, too. There will be always one zebra who stays awake on the lookout when everyone else is asleep. For wildebeest, having no central command, they will all face the same direction while sleeping standing up. This way no one will part from the herd. Tomson's gazelle are highly alert. They only sleep ten minutes the most at night.

*"Moses, I'll stay vigilant tonight, watching for spooky silhouettes. Let Hagar, Debi, and Ester sleep,"* proposes Ruth to Moses.

*"Thank you, Ruth. Could I ask you to keep an extra eye on Hagar due to her maternity condition?"*

*"Absolutely, it's my pleasure. Have you checked out our son, Joshua, lately? How is he doing?"* Ruth asks anxiously.

*"Joshua is doing fine. He is having a ball in the bachelor group. Ruth, you got to put him out of your mind. Joshua is a grown zebra. Soon, he'll have his own harem to lead and his own calves to raise. Thank goodness, we still have our own harem to belong to. The family is well and everyone is healthy. In the family each of us can be a source of nurturing support."*

*"You are right, Moses, we have been lucky so far. We have not had one casualty since the harem was formed. Fortune has favored us. Just look at the good things we have: family, health, plenty of water, above all, the year round supply of fresh grass,"* says Ruth. Her heart is filled with thanksgiving.

A full-moon shrouds the plains with silvery light. The visibility provided by the moon light although incomparable to the sun light beats total darkness. Even though the herd cannot see too well at night, they have sharp hearing. They hear the shrilly laughter of hyenas fading in and out and the roars of lions resonating across the open land. Ruth is especially alert tonight. She has the responsibility of safety for her herd. She cocks her head and tunes her ears.

At night the nocturnal carnivores such as lions, leopards and hyenas are activated. They have inbuilt-night vision. A special reflected layer on the back of their eye maximizes all available light. In the dark they can see six times better than humans. This puts them to a clear advantage while hunting for prey. In open plains where covers are hard to find, lions are exposed to be seen during day time, so they hunt at night.

When lions hunt, they hunt in group. You can have an entire pride of lions hunting together. Three hundred feet away from Ruth, a pride of lions moves towards the zebra herd behind the shield of darkness. The lions have been watching the mega-herd for sometime. In their radar, a target is selected—a sleeping zebra. Each lion takes up its position. Their strategy? Blitz. That means, they will all collectively sprint and pounce. Under the circumstance ambush chase is unnecessary.

*"I don't hear lion roar anymore, why?"* Ruth wonders. She instantly has an eerie feeling. She stretches her neck to look all around her and beyond. *"Lions! Braaay, braaay...."* As she spots the killers, she barks the alarm call loudly. The flight response is automatic and ripples trough the mega-herd in seconds. In her frenzy she kicks Hagar who didn't hear the alarm and is still asleep. By that time one lioness has jumped on Ester's rump. At the same time that the rest of herd is running away, Moses hurtles in and rears up to kick off the lions. In spite of our stallion's powerful kicks, he cannot save the hunted. Ester is finished. The lioness' canine teeth have severed her spinal cord through the back of her neck. There were just too many of lions.

# The Leopard Family

Down the southern Serengeti Plain, by a lakeside, dense shrubs and tall trees block the view and conceal their inhabitants. You would not know a leopard is hidden in the tree until you get close enough to see its paws hanging from a branch. What is the magic to make them disappear? A leopard's coat is covered with 2000 spots. Spots mimic the dapple effect of shade on vegetation. It is this leopard-cloaking device that makes them blend into the background.

Perched on a tree branch is a stunning beauty that has captured the imagination of many viewers. Her large-almond-shaped-amber eyes blink at you; her rosette-dot fur coat is stylish. Kings and queens in ancient times, wealthy elegant ladies in modern times would pay a high price for their coats. What a shame, their gorgeousness becomes their death sentence!

Leopards are notorious for their elegance and mysteriousness. They are elusive and stealthy. All of a sudden, *boom*, a leopard is in front of you. A leopard can spend an hour in stalking a prey, ever moving with the prey, looking, and making each foot-step silently. Their furtiveness is made possible by their specially built foot-pads. Those pads are surrounded by sensitive hairs that help feel exactly where to put its foot for a silent step.

Rachel, a female leopard, is resting comfortably in the warm embrace of a tree, with her chin and her belly lazily flopped on a huge branch; her four paws are dangling in mid-air. On the opposite of the branch slings a carcass that she killed earlier. Life is easy for her now. She has successfully raised tow of her three cubs to adulthood. They are Tumbo and Tumba.

Tumbo and Tumba, being young adults, aren't successful hunters like mom. They still come home to feed on mom's food supply. They simply cannot grow up in mom's presence. They have cherished the grooming and playing with mom since cub hood. That is what they continue to do in spite of Tumbo being much bigger than his mother and that Tumba is about the same size of mom.

Rachel loves her children. She worked hard to feed them and taught them and protected them, all by herself. Her mate, the male leopard, played no role in their family life. However, he patrols Rachel's territory, which is part of his territory, and chases off intruders including other leopards. Most of the time, he is a solitary big cat, remains hidden by means of camouflage.

*"Mom, come down, let's go for a walk,"* Tumbo calls to mom from the ground. He can see her tail dropping down from the tree. That was his favorite toy when he was a cub. It was also a communication tool: mom flipped its tail over its back to reveal the white underside. A signal indicating that she was not seeking prey and the cubs could follow her.

Mom hears her son's call. She misses him and worries about him. With a few leaps she descends from the tree headfirst, gracefully her forepaws land on the ground. They are happy to see each other, nuzzling and licking to show their affection just like the old days.

*"Mom, let's walk to the lake for a drink. I'm thirsty,"* suggests Tumbo.

These two stroll over a boulder and gingerly make their way to the edge of the lake nearby. Bending down to drink, the mother asks, *"Son, have you found an unoccupied land to your liking yet?"* Rachel is concerned with her son's progress in establishing a territory for a new home.

*"Not yet, so far to every place I went, I got chased out by the resident leopard. Once it spurred me a fierce fight. I nearly lost my life."*

*"What happened?"*

*"I passed through a really nice area, dotted with trees and bushes. There were lots of impalas and warthogs in the clearing. I didn't*

*think this piece of fabulous land would not belong to some leopard. Surly enough, a ferocious growl followed by a thump, in front of me was a male leopard. He looked old and decrepit. In my calculation, I thought I could win this takeover fight. I stood to the fight. Boy, did I make a mistake. This old man turned out to be the toughest I've ever seen. At his age he was still agile and acrobatic. At that moment I knew I had met my match. Had I not escaped, I would have become dead meat,"* choked with emotions Tumbo relates the event.

*"Poor thing, I am sorry to hear the bad news. Thank goodness, you didn't get killed. Your day will come. You will find your idea paradise for home. Now let's go back up to the tree to feed on the fresh kill I made this morning."*

Tumbo gorges on the carcass. After he has finished eating, his belly looks like a balloon. He kisses his mom goodbye. Somehow, in his haunch he senses this is the last kiss. He probably will not see his mom again because he has, yet, to wander afar to find his place. Rachel shares the same feeling. She hates to let go, but letting go would precipitate final stage of growing up for her children. That's just what she wants for her children. She tenderly gives Tumbo a farewell kiss, which may be the last kiss. Tumbo swiftly descends from the tree and bounds off to the thickets. Rachel from the treetop looks on her son's silhouette fading away in the sun's shimmering rays, holding in her heart the best wishes for her son's future.

Next day, part of the mega-herd strolls through the clearing two hundred feet away from where Rachel is. She recognizes this is the herd that brings her a short season of feast every year. She leaps off the tree, trots into the clearing, crouches in the tall grass, and lunges at an oncoming wildebeest. She's got a good hold of the animal, sinking her claws in to anchor her body, and then she clamps her jaws on the wildebeest's throat. All happens in just a few minutes. It was an incredible feat.

Rachel is elated with her unexpected prize. This big size of carcass can feed her and her daughter at least for four days. She must drag the carcass up in the tree if she doesn't want her prize to be swiped off by hyenas or lions. With her two forepaws straddling the carcass, she drags it through the clearing into the bush and up a tree.

Rachel is a strong, powerful leopard. This wildebeest is twice her size. Yet her exceptionally strong muscles attached to the scapula enhance her ability to climb the tree while dragging prey twice her size, an advantage that other predators don't have. As soon as she hauls the prey up into the tree, lions and hyenas appear below. The hyenas are barking and bouncing, trying to reach the prey; the lions jump on the lower branches but are unable to climb any further.

Our leopard is lying confidently on top of the tree, relaxed, not a bit disturbed by her invaders. Rachel knows she got the upper hand, a strong hold that the invaders aren't able to break in. It's only a matter of time for the hyenas and lions to give up and move off. She waits.

Rachel calls to her daughter. Leopards have a distinctive call that sounds like a wood plank being cut with a saw. The sawing sound is repeated at intervals of six minutes or so. The leopard's call allows males and females to find each other and allows territorial neighbors to keep out of each other's way as well. Other sounds that leopards make include growling when aggressive, spitting and snarling when threatened, and purring when contented. Young cubs meow to call their mother.

Her daughter, Tumba, was chasing a hare when she heard mom's call. Although fully grown, Tumba lacks mom's hunting experiences. She either spooks the prey before she gets close enough, or she chases the prey too early. So far she has been feeding on small animals like hares, squirrels and lizards. More often than not scavenging has become a necessity. She hasn't tried to find her own territory yet. She is just not confident enough at this point. Mom knows it, and mom is kind enough to allow her to hunt in her territory till she either settles down in a new home or inherits mom's home range when she dies.

Tumba is bounding towards mom who is reclining on a quarry. The ritual of greeting between mother and daughter begins: rubbing, licking and nuzzling followed by the fun of chasing each other's tail. Why not, one is never too old to have fun. After Tumba tumbles and mom's paws land on her belly, they decide to call it a day. *"Let's get back into the tree. I have a surprise for you,"* says mom.

In a few leaps and bounds, both mother and daughter are up in the tree. *"My goodness and graciousness, this is one huge carcass. How did you manage to drag it up into the tree?"* Tumba sighs with her eyes wide opened.

*"Muscles, my dear, rally your shoulder muscles when you drag. A right tree will also make a difference. Select a tree that is easy to climb. You want to avoid a straight up trunk and choose a trunk that is tilted a little bit,"* advises mom. Rachel never passes up any educational opportunity in training her children.

# The Newborns

In late January, the migration is settled in the short-grass lands on the southern plains. Game moves into the Ngorongoro Crater, the world's largest crater, which has a diameter of ten miles. It is also the season for zebra foaling.

It has been three months since the mega-herd left Maasai-Mara. Moving from eastern short-grass plains into the southern short-grass plains, the herbivores have been indulging themselves with the endless supplies of high-quality food. This nutritious food is critical for the females because most of them are pregnant. The favorable environment sets them up for a latter-stage-fat pregnancy with its plentiful, rich food. The development of the unborn depends totally on the pregnant mothers' health condition. The well-nourished females generally give birth to strong, healthy calves.

Hagar has contractions every few minutes in her entrails. She tells Ruth, *"I think the time is near. The baby is coming out soon."*

*"Can you hold it till we move into the center circle of the zebra herd?"* requests Ruth. She has a good reason to have Hagar move to the center where the crowd is: to seek safety in numbers. It is a strategy against the onslaughts on mothers and newborns by the carnivores. To get to the newborns, the carnivores will have to pass through a crowd of herbivores.

Beginning in late January, for a six-week window, the Serengeti plains are heading for one of the most dramatic events—a huge population growth. Most of the calves will be born. Every minute there will be fifty births. And the carnivores know it. The field is a smorgasbord for them. There will be so many foals, easy prey, to gobble down.

The experience of being slaughtered helplessly year after year prompts the mega-herd to give birth together during the day on the open plains. Giving birth together gives the cover over the mothers;

26

giving birth during the day will minimize night time ambushes from lions. In a nutshell, synchronizing births unto this window of timeframe on the open plains means fewer predations. Unlike human mothers who cannot control the birth process, the ungulates are able to delay birth to avoid predators, if they are not too far into labor.

Hagar and Ruth move to the center, passing numerous mothers that are in labor. Some are in the process of giving birth while standing with a bulging rear. Others have already given birth and are prodding their newborns to stand up.

Ruth stays by Hagar who's got situated. *"Push, Hagar, push, this is a good time to give birth. No spooky sign of hunters are nearby. You want to get the baby out and get it stand up before the baby-eater shows up,"* urges Ruth. These animals are living in a constant vigilance.

Gripped by contraction, Hagar starts pushing with all her strength. In a few minutes her bulging rear slithers out the amniotic sag, followed by the newborn.

*"It is a colt, we have a boy,"* Ruth shouts in excitement. She gallops off to find Moses.

Hagar licks her baby, carefully removing the fetal membranes, drying the newborn calf. This intimate touching acquaints her baby with her own smell. The first few hours are crucial for bonding between mother and baby. During this time they must get used to the smell, sight and sound of each other, so the calf can find and follow its mother. A calf that cannot identify its own mother in the herd will die of starvation or be eaten by the carnivore.

Hagar examines the calf while licking him all over. *"What a beautiful and healthy baby!"* she marvels at this little, brown and white creature. The calf is struggling on his part to look, to stand up. After all this is a new world to him, a very strange world. He raises his head up to look at Hagar's face and body. Instinctively he knows this is "mother", someone who will nurse him and shelter him. His gaze upon Hagar is filled with as much adoration as Hagar's marvel at him.

*"Come on, little one, stand up,"* Hagar says softly to the calf and gently nudges the calf's rump. The calf rises partway, then it slips, and four legs sprawl on the grass. *"Good try, my baby, let's do it again,"* prods Hagar. The little foal—inherited Moses' strong-will—with shaky legs springs back up, oops, only to fall again. After five unsuccessful attempts, finally the calf manages to stand up on its four shaky legs.

*"Follow me, little one,"* calls Hagar to her baby, while moving a few feet away. The baby wobbles towards her. *"Good job!"* exclaims the mother. By now the calf has gained confidence in itself with the mother's coaching and encouragement. The baby reaches to the mother's belly nuzzling and finds a nipple and begins to nurse. Every step of the process has been done perfectly and the whole process took only fifteen minutes. The bonding between the mother and child is underway. If the calf just stays close to its mother at all time, then he will live and thrive in the mega-herd.

Moses gallops back at top speed from the field, raising a trail of dust in his wake. He is thrilled that Hagar has given birth to a colt—his son. He wants his posterity to multiply and his gene be carried on. He takes on a father's role with his young. He trains them and protects them.

A beautiful image of a mother suckling a foal is right in front of him. He nuzzles up to give both a kiss. The baby's astonished eyes stare at him, wondering who this is. Moses makes a little dance in celebration of the event. Looking at the baby he says, *"Son, I shall call you Samuel."*

\*\*\*\*\*\*\*\*\*\*\*\*\*\*

Rebecca, the mother-to-be wildebeest, weaves between lines of grazing animals. She is moving towards the center of gathering, for she is gripped with contraction. On her way she sees wildebeest foals dropping all over the place. Wildebeest flood the market by giving births to 400,000 claves in one month, ensuring that eighty percent of them survive for the first four weeks. Despite this, predators still kill almost fifty percent of them before they are weaned.

The same drama of birth replays when Rebecca gives birth to a female calf. She welcomes the little one into her life. She is as patient as the zebra mother in guiding and assisting her calf to stand and walk. She makes sure her baby identifies her and follows her. The little one responds to mom's call and prodding and is able to stand up and walk in no time.

Unlike the stallion who takes part in the family responsibility, the father wildebeest assumes no responsibility. He only shows up during mating season. Rebecca must single-handedly raise her calf through good times as well as bad times.

Rebecca cherishes her little one, and is grateful that during the delivery both she and her baby were spared from the attacks of predators. Many others weren't so lucky. Some of the newborns were pounced on and eaten by predators even before their chance of life begins; so were some mothers, due to birth exhaustion slow in response, became prey.

The wildebeest calf is a curious little thing. She tends to wander off to check things out, and get lost. One time she got lost, and before Rebecca found her she nuzzled up to another nursing-wildebeest mother. What a shock, that mother wasn't a bit like her own mother who was forever loving and receiving. That mother charged her. She was lucky to escape the mad mother's deadly horns. Was she happy when she saw mom running to her just in time to escort her away! Will this near-disaster lesson teach her to always stay close to mom? We will find out.

Our Tomson's gazelle mom, Edith, likewise, joins the mega-herd-dramatic-birth event and gives birth to a female fawn. She is in the same predicament as our wildebeest mom, Rebecca: without the support of their mates. She is especially vulnerable because of her tiny size and light weight. However, her deficiency is compensated by her agility, speed and high sensitivity. Her survival depends on these nature-endowed abilities.

After the initial steps of acquainting with her baby through smell, sight and hearing, she urges the little fawn to stand up and walk. The little fawn manages to walk in a few minutes and to scamper in a few hours. However, mom doesn't encourage the baby to follow her. She expects the baby to stay put in tall grass during the time when she grazes in the plains, or takes a drink from the waterhole. Strange enough she won't even come to the baby's hiding place to nurse. She calls the baby to come out to her.

Edith takes the baby strolling up and down the grassland, and finds a nice den for her. Edith tucks her baby in. Born with the urge to lie down in a safe shelter, the little fawn situates herself snuggly into this clump of grasses her mother chose for her. Lying low, the little fawn disappears in the grass. The fact that the newborn has no odor makes it impossible for her to be detected by the predators through scent. If the little one just makes no noise and keeps still, she will be safe in her little den.

Not wanting to leave her own scent lingering around her baby's den to attract predators, instead of going to the den, Edith calls out her baby in a distance, *"Hello, little one, it's milk time."*

Recognizing mom's voice, the fawn leaps out, bounding towards her. Nursing is the time of bonding for them. *"Mom, when can I go with you to graze in the field?"* asks the fawn while suckling. Every child wants to go with mom; no child wants to stay home alone.

*"Soon, my child, when you are strong enough, and able to run fast. Till then you must stay still and make no sound in your den."* Edith is grateful that her child has made it so far, considering numerous fawns have been eaten by predators. They were eaten because they jumped out and fled when the predators were passing by, not even aware of their presence. Too bad! Moving targets invite predators to chase. Should they have stayed put as what their mothers have requested, they would have stayed alive.

# Half Way Round the Circle

As February turns to March, the mega-herd has completed their north to south leg of their migration. An odyssey of three-hundred-ten miles marked with tragedies as much as contentment. Many lives were taken; many new lives were born, too. The race keeps on. Will the second half of the odyssey be an easy cruising through a lush Eden, or will it be faced with the bloodiest assault yet?

The southern short-grass plains are starting to take strain due to overgrazing. Moses is galloping up and down again, looking for a new patch for his harem. With much endeavor he always finds one. This time he believes is the last time the herd will ever graze down the southern grassland. The heavy rains are approaching, harbingered by the dark clouds hanging above. The saga of Maasai-Mara replays here: too much rain, striped grasslands, and muddy mess.

Their next challenge is the long march, north through Moru Kopje and Seronera area, then towards the western corridor, back into Kenya.

Seronera is a small settlement in Serengeti National Park. It is named after the nearby river, the Seronera. The Seronera River is a permanent river, with water even during the long dry season, which flows northwest from the plains through the valley and ultimately into the Grumeti River. The river is lined with beautiful umbrella acacias, yellow barked acacias and sausage trees. Much of the ground along the banks is clad in dense vegetation. Many deep pools of water are strewn here and there. Grazing animals flock to this lush Eden for food and water. The riverine forest nearby is an ideal habitat for lions and leopards.

*"Ruth, we are leaving the Serengeti southern grasslands and heading for western corridor through woodlands. The woodlands are no fun; there could be an assailant hiding behind every tree, every bush, and every thicket. To better protect ourselves we are*

*parting from the wildebeest and gazelle herds for a better path to cross. We will be seeking our own food and water,"* Moses tells Ruth about their upcoming itinerary plan.

*"I dread this landmark. Every year when the migration enters the western-corridor woodlands, we are faced with tough terrains, starvation, and, the worst of all, drowning from crossing two rivers. We were stupid to have left Maasai-Mara,"* Ruth complains bitterly. She lays down her usual bravery and let herself be seized by fear of the unknown that is hurling at them with ferocity.

Seeing that Ruth is overcome with fear, Moses tries to encourage her and says, *"I am sorry, Ruth, you are stressed out by upcoming hardship. I understand. Perhaps with a little bit positive thinking, you'll pull yourself out of it. Just think once we have crossed the Grumeti River, the mega-herd regroups at the last pit stop the Ruana Plain. And there the clear-open savannah will be extending out before our eyes. You see,"* he continues, *"we had to leave Maasai-Mara in October when the land was drenched by heavy rains and the grasses were all cropped clean. Refusing to migrate would mean starvation."*

*"Thank you, Moses, for putting things into perspectives. You are a good leader, we will follow you."*

*"Ruth, please keep an extra eye on Hagar and the little Samuel."*

*"Yes, I will. I will double my vigilance with Samuel to pay back the negligence of mine that led to the slaughter of my sister Ester,"* murmurs Ruth who is still feeling guilty of Ester's death.

\*\*\*\*\*\*\*\*\*\*\*\*\*\*\*\*\*\*\*\*

Our fully grown male leopard, Tumbo, has made his way to the Seronera riverbank area. After a long journey, he finally settles down in an acacia tree in the riverine forest. He is in luck; he hasn't been chased out so far by another leopard. No doubt he will enjoy his prime in this piece of Africa.

From a position of power in the tree, Tumbo spots a herd of zebra grazing five hundred feet away. His sharp eyes zoom in on a youngster. This one should be an easy target. He leaps off the tree, scurries towards the field. Slinking into the high-grass bush, he moves closer to the youngster. When he is about thirty feet away, he leaps out of the grass to pounce on the calf.

Moses, our stallion, being as sharp-eyed as the leopard, sees the stealthy attack, runs up and throws himself in between the calf and the leopard. The rest of harem quickly joins in to form a circle with the calf in the middle. Our leopard bounds off, disappointed!

Tumbo counted on this meal, for he hasn't eaten for a week. The attack has made him thirsty; he trots down to the riverbank to drink. He is not alone at the riverbank. A group of Tomson's gazelle is drinking, too. The sight of a leopard spooks the gazelle. In an instant everyone dashes off except one who is at the far corner, and isn't paying attention. Tumbo pounces on this day-dreamer. He hits her like an explosion. Twisting and moaning, the gazelle tries to throw off the attacker that has fastened himself to her back. The struggle proves to be in vain. The leopard is gripping her with his incredibly sharp claws and sinking in his spiked teeth at her neck. She is finished. Tumbo straddles his front legs over the carcass and drags it toward a tree.

Before he gets to the tree, the hunger rumbles on in his stomach. Besides, the fresh smell of the carcass has gotten so irresistible, Tumbo starts tearing into the belly and munching on the meat. *Thump!* Another big cat lands in front of him. It is a hungry lioness. She wants her lion share of the carcass. Snatching up the prey, Tumbo leaps away and climbs up the first tree he sees, only to slip and fall to the ground. This tree has a straight, steep trunk. The lioness picks up the dropped carcass and runs with it. Tumbo makes no attempt to chase the lioness. She is twice his size. He lost his meal again, he is about to spit fire. This leopard has been pushed too far.

Fortunately here is a land of plenty. Endless different groups of grazing animals scatter around. Tumbo doesn't have to go too far, he sees a group of warthogs marching in a single file. His silent pads surprise the warthog family. With a swat of paw he kills one piglet. Like a flash, he dashes off with the piglet hanging in his mouth. The warthog mother screams and charges after him to no avail.

Finally, Tumbo is securely enjoying his meal in the tree. The little fat piglet is of a good size that will provide with two meals for our leopard. After finishing half of the quarry, he stores the remains in the wedge of branches. He looks down and sees a hyena drooling while staring at his spoils. The hyena has made several attempts in climbing up the tree, only to flip to the ground over and over.

Tumbo, confidently, relaxes himself on the smooth branch opposite to the one he stores the carcass remains. After a good meal, it is time for a siesta. He stretches out, and then flops down with his belly flat on the branch, chin on his paws, tail and legs dropped down. Open his mouth he yawns. He seems to take great pleasure in this simple act of inhaling-exhaling. To top it off, he broadens his jaws and sticks his tongue out. In a minute he dozes off.

Tumbo is safe and secured along with his food supply in the tree secluded by the dense leaves. He practically has no competitor for food from the top position of power. The vultures cannot see him through the density of leaves and bushes. Hyenas, lions and cheetahs cannot climb trees. This vantage point has served leopards well. That is why even though they are on the list of endangered species, they are the least endangered of the three big-cats.

************

Overlapping our leopard Tumbo's new found territory is the home range of two lionesses. They are two sisters from an old pride. After reaching adulthood, they kissed goodbye their mother and other pride members, ventured off in search of a new home. After a long journey of searching an unclaimed territory they came upon the Seronera riverbanks. It was like winning the lottery. This Eden has everything for lions: lots of game to hunt, shrub and thickets to hide, and waterholes to drink.

One of the lionesses is limping. Her leg was severed during a vicious fight with a pack of hyenas. The good hearted sister would never think of such thing as abandoning her handicapped sister. She sticks to the coalition. When hunting, she lets the handicapped sister wait in ambush as she takes on the chasing.

They can smell the herbivores in the air; they can hear the gnuing of the wildebeest in a distance. Jumping on top of a kopje, they see the arriving of the stampeding mega-herd. Bravo, the beginning of a short-season feast.

The lionesses are on their lookout post, waiting patiently till the right target shows up. It is a very small pride of only two lionesses. Given one of them is a cripple, they have to be careful. Not for long, they spot a wildebeest youngster lagging behind the other adult wildebeests. Springing up to her feet, the healthy sister descents from the kopje, bounds into the clearing, and disappears in the tall grass. The limping sister follows her to the clearing and makes a left turn towards another clump of tall grass.

The trap is set. The careless calf keeps on walking without looking, and almost stumbles over the hidden lioness. Out of blue, a lioness leaps out and jumps on the prey. The astonished calf tries to escape the lioness by running away, only to run into the other lioness waiting in ambush.

The sister with bad leg sinks her powerful claws into the calf's rump, and hangs her weight on it while the other sister jumps to the throat and cuts off the windpipe. The calf is suffocated without too much of pain.

As soon as they open up the carcass, a swarm of vultures descend from the skies. They aren't the only uninvited guests. Whereas the lionesses are gorging their lions' shares, the hyenas are standing behind waiting for scraps. Not to mention couple jackals are also there hoping for scavenging tonight. Stuffed with prime meat, our lionesses decide to leave the scraps to the bystanders. This is the season of feast; one can afford to be generous.

However, the lioness' attack spooks the mega-herd. Each is trying to come up with its own strategy to reduce casualty. Small groups are formed. They are running different directions, zigzagging to avoid killers. But this seems to have an opposite effect, for smaller groups make easier for assailants to launch assaults.

## Crossing the Grumeti River

After indulging a brief season of tall-grass grazing in the central Serengeti area, the mega-herd is on the move again, taking the cue from the skies. They see the dark clouds hovering above the horizon beyond the Grumeti River. That means it is time to cross the river.

The zebra herd arrives first at the riverbanks, followed by the wildebeest herd. The Tomson's gazelle herd, the tail end of the migration, seems to be taking the *scenic* route and has yet to arrive. Each herd will choose its own crossing point.

From a bird's eye view the Grumeti River is placid and serene, but beneath water lurks a different reality. On the surface gentle flowing waters inspire calmness and relaxation. Hidden in the pale bluish-green waters crocodiles and hippos are scattered, dotting the flat water.

Nile crocodiles are ferocious and frightening carnivores. A large Nile crocodile can reach sixteen feet long and weighs over 2600 pounds. Their powerful jaws are laced with razor-sharp teeth. A crocodile with wide-open jaws is a terrifying scene. Hippos are no less ferocious and frightening than the crocodiles. Although they are herbivores, they have a foul temper. They are extremely territorial and intolerant with trespassing. In confrontations, they can open their mouths 150 degrees, displaying the ivory of their knife-sharp tusks which is harder than the elephant's.

Led by Moses, the river-crossing veteran, the zebra herd marches to the crossing point that Moses knows best suited for a safe and short crossing. A mass of zebra assembles in the open plain by the riverbank. Zebra are good swimmers and fearless of danger lain ahead. Undaunted by the sight of the remains of carcasses washed on shore, they press on.

*"My fellow zebra, I will lead my family to plunge into the Grumeti River first. We must act fast, pushing forward, giving the crocodiles*

*ambushed in the waters no chance to launch assaults,"* addresses Moses with his head held up to view his followers and the river.

The herd wastes no time in following Moses to plunge into the river. *Plop, plop...*one by one in single file, zebra are in the water swimming towards the shore. The crossing is in full motion.

Similarly, up the riverbank at another crossing point, the wildebeest herd is assembling. The scene is a lot more chaotic than the zebra herd's. Wildebeest have no social hierarchy, no leadership. The only one rule is to stick to another wildebeest. This rule is critical when it comes to a mother and her calf.

By this time the four hundred thousand calves, born in January, are four months old. At this moment of their lives, they are faced with the toughest test yet: they bond with their mother. Will the calves follow their mothers into the river, a new and terrifying experience? Some of which will not follow. That means death for those. Most calves will follow their mothers.

In a moving mass little ones have a tendency to be separated from mothers, if not trampled. Separated pairs are running about in panic, gnuing loudly, till they hear each other's call.

Rebecca, our wildebeest new mom, and her daughter are amid the crowd. She is gnuing loudly because her daughter is separated from her. She sniffs the air, hoping to pick up her scent. All she can smell is the stench of a mass of wildebeest. She tries to listen for her call. The decibel level from hundreds of thousands of wildebeests' constant gnuing makes it impossible to distinguish her daughter's call. She has pushed her way to the four corners of the assembly area. There is no sight of her calf any where. *"Where is she?"*

Alice, Rebecca's daughter, is overwhelmed by the assembly. She has never seen so many wildebeest squished in so little square-feet area. Her eyes got huge when she sees the flowing river and says, *"Wow, with this much water we won't have to worry about drought any more."* Her mind is in oblivion when she is shoved by the crowd to an opposite direction from her mother, and is, consequently, propelled to the front line—the edge of the river.

Finally, as the crowd builds up, the pressure from the herd behind just becomes too much. Perhaps one wildebeest is accidentally bumped into the water. And the crossing kicks off. All at once hundreds of wildebeests are on their way out in the crocodile infested waters. One by one the wildebeests are lolloping into the water. The momentum is vigorous. Little Alice is knocked into the water when she is trying to pull back. Now she has no choice but to swim for her life.

A group of crocodiles has been waiting for the moment—their annual feast. As soon as the wildebeests plunge into the river, the crocodiles emerge from their deep-water ambush and swing into action. Like battle ships through the open ocean, they are closing in on their prey. Fear seizes the wildebeests. Some of them turn around to go back. Too late, the going-back passage is also blocked by crocodiles. Turning around again, the wildebeests send out loud screams of distress.

In a flash, several victims are snatched by the crocodiles and dragged into the waters. The victims are fighting a brave battle, kicking and struggling. In the end the crocodiles win the battle. They are just too powerful!

It is interesting to note how crocodiles eat their prey. Crocodiles cannot slice the meat with their teeth, their jaws are solely designed to grip and hold. Spin is the only way to tear off a mouthful. Crocodiles spin to rip off a chunk of prey's flesh, gulping it down and chew.

While all the chewing, munching and ripping, devouring are going on in the water, the Grumeti River is being dyed with blood. In addition the splashing and ripping sounds from the crocodiles and the frantic screaming from the wildebeests add to the drama. What a horrific scene!

Yet, the crossing continues. The few sacrificial lambs that have satisfied predators' hunger have allowed some tranquility for the crossing. With a full belly the crocodiles are swimming away. The crossing is then in full swinging. By the time the sun is setting, most of wildebeests have already crossed the river.

Among the very few still lingering on the shoreline, hesitating about crossing is Rebecca who is still hoping to find her daughter in the aftermath. She has sniffed every washed-ashore carcass remains to identify for her daughter. She is glad that none of which resembles Alice's scent. But, where is she? *"Is she eaten up by the crocodile in the water? Oh, no!"* groans Rebecca with anguish in her throat. Compelled by the sight of the mass of wildebeest on the opposite shore exiting the riverbank, Rebecca lollops into the river to catch up with the herd. *"Perhaps, Alice is on the other side of riverbank,"* murmurs Rebecca, desperate for a glimpse of hope.

The golden sunset is over the Grumetic River. The shimmering water mirrors the sun rays. Peace and tranquility seem to have returned to the region. Not quite, mother and daughter are, yet, to be reunited. On the shoreline, the separated pairs are desperately trying to find each other. Alice, having witnessed the horrific onslaught of the herd by the crocodiles and having swung ashore by herself, is now frightened by the entire ordeal.

*"Where is mom?"* Her anxiety knows no bound. *"Is mom drowned? I hope not."* She starts to gnu loudly in the hope that mom is still alive and will hear her call. The crowd that propelled her to the water is thinning out, and some of them have already departed from the riverbank. Standing alone on shore the little one is torn, not knowing what to do: to depart with the herd, what if mom is to show up soon; or to stay and wait for mom, what if mom is already dead?

In the nick of time a miracle happens. Mom's familiar gnuing crescendos in the distance. Alice scrambles to follow mom's sound. There, trotting in mom's hooves. These two, mother and daughter, are reunited. Here, we have a moment of thanks, thanks to the gift of life!

# The Great Pride

The Serengeti sustains one of the biggest lion populations in Africa. Approximately 3500 lions, living in 300 prides scattered in the woodlands as well as grasslands. Each pride's home range is about 10 square miles. The average pride here contains two pride males, four lionesses, and a few cubs.

Lions are the only true, social big cats. A lion pride is a social structure, a family unit where the blood-related lions live together supporting each other. Like the human family each member has a role to play, a contribution to make. The head of the family is an alpha male.

In the northwest corner of the Serengeti lies the Ruana Plain, a clear-open savannah fringed with forest and dotted with kopjes. In one of the rock outcroppings, a pride of lions takes residence and turns it to a lion den. The pride's commander in chief is an alpha male, named Dave, assisted by his brother Sal. There are five lionesses and ten cubs in the pride. They are, currently, seventeen in total. The make-up of the pride is subject to change: any adult lion can break away and leave the pride, any cub can be killed unexpectedly, and new additions are frequent with five pride lionesses. The story of the great pride is an account of how they live together, about the family affairs of one pride as their cubs struggle to grow up.

This is a prosperous pride with healthy cubs and strong adults. The pride owes its prosperity to the facts that its hunting reserve has plentiful resident animals such as zebra, impala and buffalo, and that during rainy season storm conditions draw the mega-herd to spill into the plains and add to their dinner menu. Every year the pride has two to three months of lavish feast delivered to its front door.

May arrives. In the Ruana Plain the storm season sets in. Heavy rain pours down on the plains. Overnight, following the first rain, new grass sprouts from the earth, creating a paradise for the feasting herds. The mega-herd after crossing the Grumetic River is eager to find a resting place to recuperate from the energy lost during the battling event of river crossing. Once out of the woods, to their delight a carpet of green grass is rolling out in front of them. Immediately, groups upon groups of wildebeest, zebra and Tomson's gazelle set out to crop, browse, and nibble. Each species eats their favorite part of plants in harmony with other species.

Nearby lions are perched on the lookout quarry. The quarry is located in a perfect spot to have a bird eye's view of the plains below. The lions have been watching the pouring in of the mega-herd. They seem to be in no hurry of getting down making a kill. Instead they are quite laid-back and enjoying themselves of this annual, animal spectacle.

At dusk the oldest lioness, the grandmother, gets up and descends from the quarry. Led by the grandmother the four lionesses get up to their feet, too. As the four lionesses march into the field, the grandmother strolls onto the boulders where the cubs are playing. The grandmother is in charge of the nursery. What better way to let grandmother baby-sit than to let the cubs follow moms and debunk their hunt.

This group of four lionesses each knows its strength and weakness. They hunt in cooperation. The fast runner will chase; the strong muscle will clamp down the jaws; the heavy weight will hold the prey. The one who suffocates the victim to expire is the main hunter, others are assistants.

Lions deploy a number of hunting strategies including the ambush, the blitz, or the lone hunt. The ambush takes more elaborated efforts to synchronize lions' move, but is the most common and effective strategy. The lone hunt can be effective because sometimes it's your partner who spooks the hunt. On average the group hunt has a one in three chance of capturing and killing prey, compared to the lone hunt's one in five.

The cooperating-hunting techniques are learned while living in the pride. At the age of one, cubs are allowed to run alongside the hunting ground, but not taking part in the hunt. After reaching two years old, cubs are able to hunt independently. However, not until three years old will their group-hunting skills be perfected.

The stellar hunter in this pride used to be the grandmother. Since the grandmother has retired the daughter, Miriam, has taken her place. She has mastered the art of stalk and has honed the timing of ambush. She is quick, strong and powerful. Usually she is the one that gives the victim the kiss of death. Miriam and her sister, Mamalu, are the chasers. Their cousins, Titi and Mumu, are the catchers.

All four lionesses are taking up their positions and slinking towards a group of grazing animals. The move is coordinated. If one is off her position, the other would wait for her to catch up. Their eyes are on the wildebeest herd. Tomson's gazelle are too hard to catch because they can easily outrun lions. Zebra? Oh, no. They just had a resident zebra for dinner yesterday. Voilà, three hundred feet away a small group of wildebeest zooms in to their focus. The lion group splits: Titi and Mumu move to the right, Miriam and Mamalu to the left.

One highly alert zebra detects the lionesses in the grass and tosses its head, ready to sound the alarm. Titi and Mumu quickly drop down their hunting bearings and turn round with tails up, signaling "not hunting" to the other animals. The zebra breathes a sigh of relief and keeps on grazing. The minute the zebra's head is down, the two lionesses spring to the target wildebeest and block its passage to the herd. The wildebeest turns round and runs for his life, only to be jumped on by Miriam and Mamalu waiting in ambush.

Miriam has her claws sunk in the rump of the victim. With her claws anchored, she pushes forward to reach the victim's fore-body. At first, she tries to throttle the victim's throat. She changes her strategy after the fierce struggle from the animal. Instead she puts her mouth around the wildebeest's mouth and clamps down tight so the animal cannot breathe. There, the kiss of death seals the victim's fate. The wildebeest looses its footing and is taken down by the lionesses.

Mamalu is holding down the prey when the reinforcement, Titi and Mumu, arrive. Both sink in their canine teeth. The victim stops struggling. To be on the safe side, Miriam places her paws in front of the victim's nostrils to make sure the breathing has stopped.

The rest of pride has been attentively listening for cues. Their ears swivel in the direction of sounds. The noise of struggling preludes a successful hunting. Quietness afterwards indicates that a kill is made. A dinner is ready. In no time, the two males, the grandmother, and the ten cubs are all emerging from the tall grass.

*"Wow, look at the size of this creature! Wildebeest is my favorite meat. Mom, I am almost one year old, can I come with you next time when you hunt?"* begs Lulu. The instinct to hunt and to kill arouses the cubs.

*"Yes, you and Nile, your brother, both can come with us next time."*

*"You must be very careful not to spook the prey, making no noise, no disturbance. Run alongside of Miriam and pay attention to her every move,"* the grandmother nags.

The males, not taking part of the hunt, bustle in to claim the prize. *"What a fat carcass! This will provide plenty of meat for everyone to stuff themselves to death. Tonight the pecking order is abolished at the dinner table,"* says the jolly alpha male.

The great pride gorges noisily its first seasonal feast. Lions, being at the top of the food chain, have no fear of being seen eating, smack food in their mouths with loud roars and grunts. In contrast, vulnerable cheetahs eat quietly for fear of being found out by other predators.

The pecking order at the dinner table privileges the alpha male to eat first and have the choice meat, followed by other males, then adult females. The scraps are left for the cubs. When food is plentiful, the pecking order is often overlooked; when food is scarce, the pride alpha male, the power, dominates the food source.

Although cubs are the last to eat, the alpha male often permits little cubs to eat with him. It makes sense because little cubs eat very little and eating together enhances bonding. Cubs are adult lions' future. Like humans, the young, when fully grown, takes care of the elderly: feeding them, sheltering them, and protecting them.

***************

Dave, the pride-alpha, is an impressive five-hundred-fifty-pound, with a sumptuous black mane running round his face, neck, and all the way to his abdomen. He and his brother Sal are the fathers of all the cubs in the pride. Sal has a golden mane and is as handsome as his big brother. These two brothers departed from their old pride once they reached adulthood. They traveled together in search of a new homeland. Wandering carries the risk of trespassing in someone else's territory. They were battled and chased off over and over by other pride males for intrusion. Not until they came upon a group of lionesses did they receive a warm welcome. These males and females quickly set out to form a pride.

No sooner had the pride settled down than the females started to get pregnant and began to give birth. The pride population exploded. If it weren't for the high death rate at birth, the pride would have fifteen cubs today. Now with seventeen members in the pride, they are a great pride.

Dave and Sal are proud of their cubs who carry their genes. They aren't as attentive as the lionesses to the cubs, but they stick around and put up with the cubs' game play and foolishness. They take part in cubs rearing and family bonding. Their devotion to the lionesses and the cubs compels them to lay down their lives to defend the family.

To protect their family is to secure their territory. Dave and Sal together patrol the territory by scent-marking, spraying their urine onto shrubs and scraping dirt to ensure that the scent lasts. They often roar for hours to proclaim the ownership of the land to ward off intrusion. Their roar can be heard as far as five miles away. Most animals respect lions and do not cross them, except hyenas.

Hyenas and lions are eternal enemies. Since they hunt for the same prey, they are locked in a constant clash for food and territories. Hyenas are ferocious and aggressive predators. Their large, powerful jaws are deadly. Hyenas' bite force is one thousand pounds, second to Nile crocodiles. Their jaws crush victim's bones. *Crunch, crunch,* in a few minutes the entire carcass is consumed. Physically hyenas are smaller than lions. Power is balanced by hyena clans' team work. When the clan numbers are great, lions can be in serious danger.

Our pride's territory overlaps with a clan of hyenas. During the time that the lion pride was enjoying its prosperity and tranquility, the hyena clan was going through some internal turmoil. The alpha female was dethroned by her own daughter. The crowned princess was killed by the same daughter in the butchery. Now the lion pride has a new alpha hyena to deal with.

Hyenas live in a highly intelligent social network. They are organized into territorial clans of related individuals. As in all intelligent social species, the hierarchy and bonds between animals in the clans require sophisticated communication skills. Indeed, hyenas have an incredibly rich vocal repertoire of calls—fourteen sounds—that they use in communication. The best known hyena call is the hoot-laugh, or giggle which has led humans to designate these animals as "laughing hyenas."

In hyena society it really matters what sex you are and who your mother is. Female cubs of high ranking mothers inherit their status. Female hyenas are dominant over the males and outweigh them by about three pounds. The most dominant female, an alpha female, reaches her top status through challenge fights. Once power is secured it can be handed down to the alpha queen's child. The alpha queen has a favorite daughter. She gets to inherit the mother's throne. She is the crowned princess. Like her mother, she receives respect from the rest of the clan. That being said, power struggle is common among siblings. A hyena's most dangerous enemy is not the lion rather its sibling. Yet hyenas love to challenge lions.

During Dave's patrolling routine, the newly crowned alpha female shows up and follows Dave's every step. To show off her guts she taunts Dave. Dave sprays the urine; she sprays her urine, too. Dave kicks dirt; she kicks dirt, too. The mimicking is absolutely disrespectful. The hot tempered Dave turns round and lunges at her. Fortunately, she is agile enough to escape the pounce. With a hysterical *yelping*, the hyena queen runs for her life. Dave, by now an angry lion, is relentlessly pursuing on her tail. The chase is on. Before long the alpha female trips and tumbles. Dave runs up and snaps her throat. Poor thing, the newly crowned queen taunted Dave because she thought she could outrun Dave. She would have outrun Dave hadn't it been for that one fatal trip.

On top of hyenas Dave and Sal have rival prides to deal with. Lion prides' territories border each other. Encroachment, trespassing, intrusion—all are not tolerated and can flare up temper and lead to fights.

The neighbor pride at the northeast corner occupies a smaller than average home range. The pride is growing. The two pride males are trying to expand their territory by encroaching upon Dave and Sal's. First, the two males scent-mark beyond the border line. It means they would urinate on top of Dave and Sal's signature scent-mark to claim the land. Dave and Sal are offended by this defiant act. They reclaim the turf by renewing scent-marks on top of their rivals'. It is only a matter of time for the dispute to erupt into a brawl.

Lions' territorial fights have several different types of tactic from posturing to a physical fight. The least violent form is a sort of posturing in which two males sit a few feet apart, face-to-face, and stare at each other. The first one to break his stare is the loser. Usually lions try not to escalate the territorial dispute into a bloody fight. They know better that a bloody fight could lead to death. If not death, injury. An injured lion is undesirable because it cannot hunt.

When Dave patrols up to the northeast corner of his pride's territory, he smells again the rival's scent. He bristles with anger. Guess what, the perpetrator is not too far. Only one hundred feet away, the rival pride male is spraying in Dave's territory. With a ferocious roar Dave charges the rival. He hunches his back, widens his shoulders, and shakes his mane to make himself look big and tough. If this doesn't impress the rival, he rears up and swipes the air with both paws.

In response, the rival lion flaunts his canine teeth, and swats the air with his paws, too. However, both sides are reluctant to engage in a physical fight. By dramatizing their posturing, each hopes that its adversary will give in and retreat. No one is giving in. That evens up a standoff…Not until Sal, the reinforcement, hurries in does the rival lion turns round and retreats. A bloody fight is avoided, but the border dispute isn't resolved.

Rival-male lions are pesky; nomadic-male lions are deadly. The nomadic lions are the ones who do not have a home land. They wander around in search of an unclaimed land to establish their territory. Sometimes, they take up a land occupied by another pride through a takeover fight. The takeover fight is fierce and bloody. This is when the alpha male—as pledged—will lay down his life to protect his lionesses and cubs. If not, the nomadic lions will kill the cubs sired by the pride males. Then, when the lionesses go in estrus again, they will mate to have cubs sired by their own genes.

Dave and Sal are thankful that there hasn't been any takeover attempt launched by nomadic lions. They keep their claws crossed. Will the great pride be spared from the takeover attempt down the road? Time will tell.


\*\*\*\*\*\*\*\*\*\*\*\*\*\*

After patrolling Dave and Sal head back to the lion den and join the rest of the family for a siesta. Lions sleep and rest twenty hours a day. It is not hard to find the pride huddling together in a confused jumble of paws, heads and tails and dozing off. The cubs are more active. Little rambunctious cubs, if not suckling, climb up and down mom's back, chase mom's tail. Juveniles, bristled with energy, chase each other up and down rocks or up and down trees.

A snapshot of this family is a happy one. The story behind the family is like a fairy tale. The grandmother wedded her prince of charming and gave birth to five cubs. One male cub died from intestinal infection. The four surviving female cubs grew up to be four strong and healthy lionesses. The grandmother used to be a stellar hunter. She has passed her skills on to her four daughters. Later, daughter Miriam has excelled the hunting skills and has surpassed that of mom's. Two years ago the grandfather was injured in an attempt to jump on a buffalo, and eventually died of the nasty wound. Just when there was no man in charge of the house, Dave and Sal showed up. They were received warmly by the girls. Thus the great pride was born.

All five lionesses gave birth to a total of fifteen cubs. Three of them died at birth. Two of them died young from disease. Now, Miriam has two cubs; Mamalu three; Titi two; Mumu two; Grandmother one. Miriam and Grandmother's cubs are teenagers. They are weaned and are eating meat. Mamalu, Titi, and Mumu's cubs are still nursing.

Like human family, a lion pride is governed by love, affection and support. Pride members are primarily blood related, but some prides do adopt outsiders to become pride members. They enjoy each other's companionship and display their feelings through greeting and grooming. Rubbing and licking enhance their relationship. There are scent glands on the corners of their mouth. The scent will be deposited on the other lions during rubbing and licking. In addition, male lions will spray other lions as a means of bond strengthening.

The family system allows cooperation in rearing the young. Lioness moms watch out for each other's cubs. The nursing cubs can go to mom or aunts for suckling. Cubs' rough-and-tumbles at play time establish family ties. Equally important is that it prepares the skills they will need in hunting later on. This form of nurturing and teaching the young makes the pride viable.

**************

*"Mom, are you leaving for a hunt? Last time you said I could come with you to hunt, "* asks Lulu, the teenage girl. She is restless in the lion den. She has been helping Grandma watching her little cousins. By now she is bored with their rough-and-tumbles. She wants the real thing—to take part in real action, to hunt like an adult lioness.

*"I guess so. Then, both you and your brother Nile come with us. You must pay close attention to cues. When we duck, you duck; when we crawl, you crawl. Do all these with stealth, not to alarm the prey. You know there are lookout sentries every where. Birds and baboons in trees, zebra and gazelle in plain fields—all are ready to blow our covers the minute we spook them, "* lectures Miriam.

*"I promise, mom, "* says Lulu.

*"I promise too, mom, "* says Nile.

The four lionesses rise from the cool boulders and pad down the rock hills. This time the hunting group is joined by two excited adolescent cubs. When Miriam passes by the two adult males, she nudges their shoulders to gesture them to join the hunt. Neither one is interested in. Both males keep on dozing off and leave hunting tasks to the females. Might as well, for male lions are lousy hunters. Their huge manes give them away. Animals spot them easily. For them to sneak up on prey is practically impossible. Their heavy weight makes them clumsy. Oops, never say never, sometimes their clumsiness is rewarded when heavy weight is required in taking down heavy prey like buffalo.

*"Sons, first thing in hunting is to select a target. Your target should be within three hundred feet, "* says Miriam.

Like cheetahs, lions aren't able to chase prey very long, only few seconds. Their stocky bodies are designed for the sprint and pounce of the ambush attack. To ensure success, Miriam must stage the ambush as close as possible.

Miriam turns to her son and daughter and says, *"See, three hundred feet away there is a group of wildebeest grazing. Select one that appears to be sick and old."*

*"Yeah, I see one who looks old and has a wound in his rump,"* says Lulu in excitement.

*"Come on, team; let's sneak up on the old guy."* Miriam makes eye contact with the other lionesses.

*"We'll do our belly walk till we get as close as possible to the herd, like within thirty feet,"* whispers Miriam to Lulu and Nile.

Lulu and Nile follow every one of mom's instructions. They have been advancing inch by inch, crawling on their belly. One zebra looks in their direction suspiciously and tosses its head, and Miriam freezes right away. The cubs also freeze. The zebra sees no danger and continues to browse. Now the zebra heads the opposite direction to feed. Miriam and cubs advance further more. Just about thirty feet away from the target, Titi and Mumu split to the left.

*"Onslaught!"* Miriam and Mamalu burst out a loud roar and leap out to charge the target animal.

Lulu and Nile stand by and look on keenly. They were told not to jump on the animal because they can get seriously injured by the struggling animal's frantic kicks. They see the victim take the bait and run towards the ambush—the death trap. They run along side Miriam and Mamalu. When the victim is trapped Miriam springs to the victim's throat and sinks her canine teeth to crush its windpipe. Another victory for Miriam!

The carcass is ready to be opened and eaten. There is a ritual to follow, something having been passed down from generation to generation. Lulu and Nile have seen it done before but have never done it. Miriam signals Nile to come over to learn how to open the carcass, but he shies away and hides behind Lulu. Lulu is eager to learn. She advances up to the carcass, only to be pushed away by Miriam.

*"Lulu, let your brother do this. He needs to become bolder and more enthusiastic."*

Miriam nudges Nile into action. Nile looks at the carcass. He can see everyone's eyes are on the soft part of the belly. He sinks in his canine teeth, tears into the skin, and pulls the contents out. He throws out the stomach, which is to be buried, not to be consumed.

*"Good job!"* praises Miriam and gives Nile a big hug.

\*\*\*\*\*\*\*\*\*\*\*\*\*\*

A young lioness, a stranger, is passing by the great pride's territory. She was driven out of her old den along with her brothers because they were fully grown. Fully grown cubs are a nuisance to pride adults; they are usually kicked out of their pride. Now she is cast adrift in a sea of unfamiliarity to find her own niche. She'd rather ramble off seeking something different than forming a pride with her brothers. She has been scavenging, killing small animals, and eating ostrich eggs to survive. This moment she is upon Dave's turf and she is in estrus.

The sky is clear, air is balmy, and wild flowers are blooming all over the plains. Dave sniffs spring in the air. He gets up, arches his back, stretches and yawns. He pads down to the field for a walk. Dave's black mane is undulating in breezes. He strolls up to a shrub to sniff for scent. Suddenly, out of no where a lovely lioness pops in and walks up to him, to give him a kiss on the cheek.

*"Wow, what is this! Who are you and what are you doing here?"* asks Dave in shock.

*"Call me Angel. I saw your black mane flapping in wind. I am attracted to black manes. I'd like to know you. I have departed from my old pride and am looking for new friends,"* replies Angel with a sweet voice.

*"Welcome, Angel, to my territory. I would like to have you in my pride; you will always be under my protection,"* says Dave with a gallant gesture.

*"Oh, thank you. It is very sweet of you to be so gallant,"* replies Angel with love in her eyes.

It is love of first sight for these two. A young lioness adores a mature-black-mane lion, and an affectionate male loves females. The feeling is tangible. After a very short introduction, a romance is about to unravel. Wait a second…just when they are nuzzling, Miriam appears.

*"What is going on here? Stop it, he is our man!"* Miriam shouts at Angel.

Bewildered Angel didn't expect this and slinks away.

*"You, what are you trying to do? Don't you know we have gotten enough cubs to raise?"* Miriam yells at Dave in anger.

*"Calm down, we can talk about this later on,"* Dave shouts back. He is torn. He wants to follow Angel, his new found love, but he can't do it. At least not now, the madness is engulfing Miriam. Dave knows better not to get in trouble with Miriam. Perhaps later on when Miriam cools off, he can go to look for Angel.

Next day Dave sets out to find Angel. He finds her in the crevice of a rock outcropping nearby. The two lovers are happy to see each other. Kissing, hugging and playing, they are ready to mate.

When lions mate they neither hunt nor eat. They concentrate on each other. A female will be in estrus for four to eight days. To ensure pregnancy they must mate as many times as possible. A pair of lions can mate forty times in a day. Each cycle lasts about twenty minutes.

Dave takes one-week leave absence from Miriam to be with Angel. After hormone is dissipated, hunger sets in. Having enough of mating, Angel strolls away to find something to eat. Dave, duty-bound by his commitment to the pride, is headed for the lion den.

Things are back to normal in the pride. Dave is back with Sal, his lionesses, and the cubs. As for Angel, she is pregnant. She will need support after cubs are born. She also misses Dave. The only way for her to get support and to be with Dave is to join the great pride. That being said, the question is: Will the great pride accept her?

## The Mating Season

It is June. The mating season or rut is here. In the Serengeti plains food has become the secondary occupation. During a three-week period, driven by testosterone and high spirit, the sexually excited bulls start territorial skirmishes to defend their patch of ground, and round up females.

Smaller breeding groups of about one-hundred-forty animals form within the massive herds. In these small groups, five or six of the most active bulls establish and defend territories in which females are gathered.

*"Hello, beautiful, my name is Jack. I am a Serengeti veteran. I have circled the Serengeti plains five times. I have battled ferocious lions, kicked marauding hyenas, and sent off helping leopards. Look at the scars on my chest and shoulders,"* brags Jack, a big bull, to a group of female wildebeests.

*"Jeez, let me see. These are nasty gashes. You must have fought bravely,"* sigh the girls admirably.

*"You bet. Those lions maybe strong, but when I thrust my horns they all recoil and flee. Often tables are turned. I end up chasing the lions,"* encouraged by the girls' awes Jack boasts further.

*"We would like you to be our protector, if you wouldn't mind,"* petition the girls. By now the overwhelmed girls have no doubt that Jack is the one they should follow.

*"My pleasure to be at your service, my ladies,"* Jack says, *"rest assured that I will defend you and kick out any intruder. Just stay in this patch of ground that I share with my fellow bulls."*

The bulls go through all kinds of shenanigans, galloping and bucking around their territories to impress females. When wildebeest buck around, they leap with arched back and land with head low and forelegs stiff. They paw the ground and rub their heads on it, spreading secretions produced by the periorbital and interdigital glands to signal to other bulls to stay away.

When neighboring bulls step off lines and cross the boundaries of their territories, it is viewed as a provocation, and is dealt with a brawl.

Jack spots a bull from another group who strains his neck to look at his females, and steps over the edge of his territory. He immediately rushes up to challenge the bull. Aiming at the intruder, he paws the ground, bucks around, and starts to snort loudly. The intruder takes the cue—Jack wants a fight. The intruder immediately takes up his combat position on its knees, facing Jack, with its forehead flat on the ground.

*Clunk, clunk....* Sparks fly in the air. The clashes of the horns take center stage in this duel. Jack and his adversary knock each other's head and hit at the base of the horns. Their curved horns are locked. Stubbornly they push on till both are totally exhausted and finally part. No one is injured. It seems to be there is no winner, no loser just an exuberant show to impress ladies.

On the part of the bulls they must act aggressive in getting females because they are on a strict time table. Females only come into estrus for one day within their three-week period. This window of synchronized mating sows its seeds for 400,000 new arrivals next January. Calving all at once provides enough food for carnivores to feast on, and there will be plenty left to ensure the survival of each herbivore species. It is a strategy which increases the species' viability through safety in numbers.

# The Cheetah Family

It is July. By now the cheetah family's three adolescents have gotten enough hands-on lessons on hunting. The cheetah mom has trained them well for independent lives. A diligent tutor would cement the foundations of all cubs' hunting skills. Yet they don't appear to be enthusiastic about living independently. They are more than happy to let mom do all the work while they indulge themselves in foolish game play.

*"Come, kids, the kill is made,"* Eve is chirping in the field to call her boys and girl to eat. A large size of impala is taken down. Eve sits down panting to catch her breath. Cheetah's light weight body is designed for a short burst of high speed chase. And it cannot last for more than one minute. Going overboard would set off instant death. That's why many times after a minute if the prey is still running, Eve stops chasing. Her success rate in catching the prey is one in five.

In no time all three emerge from the grass, trotting towards the carcass. Pleased by what they see, they blurt out, *"Mother, you are wonderful. We knew we could count on you. You would never let us go hungry."* Three kids have such sweet mouths that butter and sugar wouldn't melt in them.

*"Okay, my children hurry to eat your dinner while I am on guard for scavengers."*

Vultures are always the first scavengers to show up because they can spot carcasses way up in the sky. For other predators they are the towering beckons. Smart hyenas and lions would look up in the sky and follow the vultures' flying direction to where the carcass is located.

A swarm of vultures are descending from the sky and is closing in on Eve, her cubs, and the carcass. Eve sweeps the vultures off and keeps them at bay. One bold jackal pushes his way in and swipes off a small piece of meat. *Munching, munching,* the cheetah family continues on feeding. Just when the carcass is pretty much cleaned up, hyenas are moving in from all directions.

*"Hey, kids, let's get out of here. The big guys are here. We aren't going to waste our energy battling with them."* Eve sends out a retreat signal. The cheetah family dashes off.

Back to the cool shady spot under the tree, the cubs resume their rough-and-tumble, whereas Eve is thinking, *"What should I do to get my kids to mature, to become responsible? By now they should have lived independently, but none of them wants to part, none of them takes part in any work... I know what I can do."* A light bulb is lit in her mind.

Next day, the cheetah family's athletic, young adults decide to play something new: to have a contest to see who can jump to the highest point of trees in their surroundings. Unlike leopards whose paws are equipped with sharp claws, cheetahs' front paws are equipped with splayed hooves. Cheetahs aren't designed to climb trees. They will have to look around for trees that have low branches for them to jump on. After much horsing around, they got hungry and start to head for home.

When they return to their usual lie-up under a big umbrella tree, they are met with an empty den and an eerie calm. Strange, the familiar silhouette of mom lying under the tree is not there.

*"Where is mom?"* the cheetah sister, Mara, asks her brothers nervously. She has a sinister hunch.

*"She is probably getting our meal somewhere in the middle of the field. She will call us soon,"* replies brother Sango.

Evening is approaching. There is still no sign of mom. When night falls, the kids are scared. So far they haven't spent a night without mom. Panic stricken, they can hardly fall asleep.

When morning comes, they stretch their neck, hoping to see mom's silhouette emerging from the grassy fields. After a all-day-long nervous waiting, they are flustered by still-no-sign-of-mom. These kids aren't playful anymore. Worry sinks in.

*"Perhaps, mom is eaten by lions,"* says Mara in a shaky voice.

*"Nope, Mom is the fastest runner on the planet. Lions are no match,"* asserts Sango. *"Anyway we'll have to go out to hunt by ourselves tomorrow in case mom doesn't show up by then."* His voice is just as trembling.

*"We are going to die. We have never hunted without mom's help. We are unable to make a kill,"* sobs Natron in fear.

*"Courage, my brother, have courage. Three of us make a formidable team. I assure you. We are able to make a kill. We'll prove it tomorrow,"* consoles Sango to his brother.

*"That's right, Natron, we'll work as a team and will make a kill tomorrow. Now let's go to sleep,"* says Mara to her brother.

The cubs spend another day of waiting, fretting and hoping. Still no sign of mom.

On the third day at dawn, our cheetah-family cubs get up and set out to hunt the first time in their lives without their mom. Trepidation grips all three. They look intently at the field where a group of impala is grazing. They look at each other to consent the intended target. Like lightening, all three take off and whip through the field. Alarm causes ripple through the herd. Herd animals scamper in all directions. The aimed animal senses itself being the target, picks up its spindle legs, and runs for its life.

Sango leads in the race. His flexible spine curves up and down as he runs… till the target is within reach. Just when he tries to trip the impala's hind-leg, the animal makes a sharp turn. At first it looks like the cheetahs have lost their game. What you know, the animal's sharp turn sends itself right into Natron's arms. Natron is running right behind Sango. Once the prey is taken down, Mara arrives in time to help hold it down. Team work scores a victory.

Not having eaten for three days, the young adults gorge their carcass in frenzy. After having been stuffed to death, they walk away leaving the craps to vultures and jackals to feed.

On their way home, even though their tummies are contented, their spirits are down. They can't help feeling sad that mom has disappeared and probably would never come home. As if they didn't have enough problems, a stranger appears in a distance. The stranger sits two hundred feet away, watching them approach.

*"Watch out, Natron and Mara, mom said something about being on guard against strangers. This cheetah who sits and watches us over there could be an intruder who is trying to steal our land."* Sango halts his walk and warns his brother and sister.

All three switch to defensive modes: ears flat, tails down, advancing cautiously. Their muscles are tense, ready to put out a good fight in defending their homeland. Trespassing is not tolerated in one's backyard.

When the cubs are close enough to see who it is, the stranger chirps. That familiar chirping sound of mom! It is mom! Mom is home! *Bravo,* the three young adults cheer and become little cubs again, scrambling to kiss and hug mom. A happily reunited family is cuddling again under the umbrella tree.

Eve repeats her disappearing and reappearing acts couple more times till she finally disappears for good. The transformed young adults act out their independent lives by making kills together. They have proved to be a superb coalition.

The coalition lives happily together until one day the young female, Mara, is acting restless. She is now a matured cheetah female and wants to breed. She has run into a handsome cheetah who wants to marry her. She is torn between to stay with her brothers or to elope with her boy friend. Brother Sango senses his sister's mood swing.

*"Mara, you are edgy. What is bothering you?"*

*"I'm sorry Sango. I have something to tell you. I love both you and Natron very much, but I have my own life to pursuit, my dream to fulfill. I want to have my own family and have babies."*

*"That's understandable. Go ahead, my dear sister, go to follow your dream. Just don't forget to visit us once a while."*

Joyful and relieved, Mara kisses her brothers goodbye and dashes off to meet her boy friend. Pretty soon Mara will have her own cubs to raise. She will remember all that her mom taught her and will pass it on to her children. The brother team will continue and thrive. Our cheetah mom, Eve, has successfully raised her three cubs to adulthood. That the young adults are not only surviving but thriving is a consolation to Eve.

# The Crisis in the Great Pride

August is here. Angel is getting very pregnant. She has found a well-hidden spot in the crevice of a large boulder for her newborns. This crevice is underneath the roof of another piece of flat rock with crawling plants hanging down to shelter the entrance. The place is rainproof and secluded from the outside world. Risk is minimized for newborns. All she needs now is the support from the pride. For a single mom to raise cubs in the Serengeti without support, the undertaking is fraught with difficulties if not danger for both mom and cubs.

Angel must seek acceptance from the great pride. She heads for the great pride den, and spots Dave perching on the quarry. Who can miss his sumptuous black mane? Elated and consumed by joy, Angel runs up to Dave stepping over the great pride members that are with Dave. Her focus was on Dave; everything else was blocked out. Dave is extremely pleased to see her. Not so for Miriam. She puts on a grumpy face and growls at Angel. Not wishing to antagonize Miriam, Angel backs off and runs away. But Miriam won't quit, relentlessly on Angel's tail chasing. In view of the hostile chasing, Dave kicks off his *whuuu, whuuu,* calling for peace. Everyone in the pride is perturbed till Dave speaks up:
*"My dear brother and my lionesses, you just witnessed an ungracious scenario. We, the great pride, chased away a friendly lioness who was seeking acceptance from us. We could have accepted her on the ground that fortune has favored us and enabled us to live a fat life. We lions are affectionate, let's show our affections, and be sensitive to the need of others. We should share what we have with love."*

Miriam is flustered by Dave's speech. Now she feels bad about chasing Angel away. *"I let my jealousy take control of me,"* Miriam confesses, *"I hope she will come back."*

Back in her den, Angel is pacing up and down nervously. She suffers a psychological blow as a result of being chased away by Miriam.

The memory is fresh. She will have no audacity to test again for acceptance. But there is a magnet drawing her to belong to a pride. This pull is so powerful that she can't help but surrendering. She finds a reason to go back.

*"Wait a minute, isn't Dave the boss in the pride? I heard him calling for peace when Miriam chased me. Perhaps, spurred by Dave's calling for peace Miriam, now, has change of heart."* With renewed hope she summons her courage and heads for the great pride again.

When she steps into the great pride's lie-up, all eyes are staring at her. Her lumpy belly reveals the secret of her pregnancy. Dave walks up and gives her a big lick. So is Miriam who licks her on the cheek. One by one all the pride members walk up to hug Angel and receive her warmly. To join the merriment the little cubs climb over her back and chase her tail. Angel, an outsider, is accepted into the great pride. The unraveling of this love story in the midst of the wilderness, where brutality rules and unforgiveness governs, is utterly heartwarming.

Belonging to a pride has many fringe benefits. On account of Angel's pregnancy condition, the pride allows her to eat without taking part in hunting. So she eats a lot for her and the babies. When time is near, she moves quietly to her chosen hideout and waits.

In a glorious day, a call for celebration of life, Angel gently eases a litter of three cubs into the world: one female and two males. The cubs are born blind. Their eyes do not open until roughly a week after birth. They weigh in two to four pounds at birth and are almost helpless. The cubs begin to crawl for a day or two after birth and from there will continue to grow into magnificent big cats in case all goes well. The miracle of these new lives adds another chapter to the saga of the great pride.

A mother lioness keeps her cubs away from the pride for six to eight weeks for fear of accidental injury caused as much by young cubs' rough-and-tumble as by adults' clumsiness. After six to eight weeks, the mother will lead her boisterous cubs to meet the pride members. Once introduced, cubs may suckle any lactating female. This helps bond the cubs to the adults, and promotes survival. The mother carries the young cubs around by the scruff of their necks when it becomes necessary to move them.

Angel is ecstatic with her babies. She meticulously licks them up clean, and does it continually leaving no speck on the cubs. Her teats are swollen with milk after herself being fed by the abundant supply of prey. She lies down to nurse her cubs all day long except, at times, she gets up to join the pride to feed. These cubs are her bundle of joy. But just when things are going Angel's way, a tragedy strikes.

Two nomadic lions are roaming in the vicinity. When they stroll passing by the lion den, they perceive a number of lionesses perching on the flat rocks. Dave and Sal are away patrolling at the far end of their territory. Most likely they will not be back till after dusk, or even till next morning. The absence of male lions encourages the nomads to win over the lionesses. Sometimes, to win over lionesses can turn to violence.

*"Brother, I see no male lions, but do you see any cub around?"* asks Beau.

*"No, I only see four lionesses, but we need to sniff around, making sure there're no signature scent-marks. The guy could be out patrolling,"* answers Bobo.

Beau and Bobo sniff around; Dave and Sal's urine is detected.

*"Brother, we got to find the cubs and kill them now,"* utters Beau with urgency. Obviously he is plotting a takeover attempt, trying to take advantage of the absence of the males. No doubt the two nomads are opportunists.

Angel's little cubs are meowing for mom in their cradle. Angel left to the waterhole for a drink. Before she left, she tucked her cubs in the deep recess of the crevice. However, two of them have already crawled out of the crevice. Led by the cubs' meowing the nomads hurry to the direction of sounds and find the two cubs.

Their murderous eyes look intensely at the cubs. Both move in quietly. Abruptly, each pounces on the intended target. One swipe, the cubs are severely wounded. In the nick of time, Angel returns from her drink. She is horrified by the scene. Enraged, she lunges at the two big males. A melee ensues. The nomads decide to retreat since they have achieved their goal, leaving a mad lioness on the trail chasing.

Badly mauled, Angel returns to her cubs. The two wounded cubs are struggling for their lives. The mother licks their deep gashed wounds, hoping to bring about healing. She lies down to nudge them to suckle. They are in severe pains and have lost the appetites. The well-cub indulges itself with profuse milk. Angel licks her own wounds inflicted in the brawl. Her tail jagged with tooth marks and her body covered with bruises, yet she would take on this fight all over again just to defend her babies.

At this hour, Dave and Sal are at the far end of their territory patrolling and proclaiming. *"Wuh-ooow, wuh-ooow, this is our land. We proclaim this territory. Let there be no trespass. Trespassers will be punished."* Together they roar and roar for hours to get their message across. However, the warning has fallen on deaf ears. Ironically, their roaring has served their enemies.

*"Listen, brother, the owners are roaring and proclaiming. Their roaring is coming in faintly. Hah, their distance is revealed! They are too far away to get back in time to battle us. We better take advantage of this hour and launch a takeover attempt at the lionesses,"* Beau urges again.

*"No, brother, we better try a more peaceful approach. Let's woo them over first,"* replies Bobo.

Whereas the lionesses are listening contentedly their mates' proclamation, the two nomads sneak up the outskirt of their lie-up and start wooing. All of a sudden, the faint roar of their mates in the distance is replaced by a rigorous roar of wooing of two males nearby. The lionesses are stunned. They swivel their ears to hear again and realize a takeover attempt is underway. Together all five lionesses roar back to say *NO* to the suitors.

*"Brother, we are rejected. That leaves us no other option except to take it by force,"* Beau utters with a cracking voice.

*"Two against four, chances are pretty good. We can win this battle. Let's go,"* agrees Bobo with confidence.

Like gangsters, the nomads close in on the lionesses. The sinister looks on their faces are calculated to scare off the lionesses to surrender. To the opposite effect, the lionesses are enraged. Everyone's adrenaline is kicked up. The lionesses are in for a fight. They know who these gangs are, a bunch of bums, and worst of all they are cub killers. Even the grandmother joins in the fight.

*"Nobody messes around with Miriam,"* spitting and spattering, *"watch out, guys, I'll give you a run for your money,"* Miriam warns at the advancing nomads. In a frantic and confused brawl of biting, swatting, mauling and hairs flying, the two macho gangsters are badly beaten up. The five lionesses, including the grandmother, prove to be some tough cookies. Had better think twice before picking on these girls.

The test of strength is attested to be a fiasco for the nomads. The girls trumped the boys. Humiliated, they scramble off and vanish into bushes. The lionesses huddle together to lick each other's wounds and console one another saying:

*"These two bad guys will not return. We have flexed our muscles and demonstrated our strength. We will join our force, stick together for the sake of our children."*

Next morning at dawn, Dave and Sal are back from their far-end patrolling. They smell a foreign odor in air. Quickly they sniff the ground and cry out, *"Intruders! We have been invaded by intruders!"* They nervously scout about to see if they can catch sight of the intruders. It looks like they missed out a big fight. Had they been here when the nomads came, they would have torn into those bandits and sent them off yelping.

Now, all is calm. The danger is over, thanks to the lionesses. Dave and Sal regain serenity when they find their lionesses and cubs are safe and sound. The nomads were chased away, the crisis is over, and tranquility returns to the lion family. To celebrate their victory, the pride greets each other with bundles of affectionate kisses and hugs

*"Wait a minute, where is Angel, is she all right, and what about the little cubs?"* asks Dave anxiously.

*"We don't know. She and the little cubs are still in the hideout. Last time we saw her at feeding time, she was all right,"* replies Mamalu.

Dave sets out to check on Angel. One can never be too careful. Upon entering her nursery, he hears her crying. He sees her moaning over the stiff, cold bodies of her babies. The little ones didn't make it through the night. The wounds were too nasty. Sadness engulfs Dave. The most heart-wrenching loss for parents is the death of their children. That both lions and humans share the same feelings. To console Angel as well as to protect her from further harm, Dave stays with her till she gets well.

Another week has passed. Sola, Angel's only survival cub, is six weeks old. Angel decides to introduce Sola to the great pride at an earlier time. Still gripped by fear, she seeks out safe haven for her only child. The sooner the better. Trotting beside mom, little Sola is to meet lions other than her mother the first time.

Sola halts her pitter-patter-little paws when the great pride comes into view. Seven adult lions and ten cubs are sprawling. The younger cubs are frisky about playing game. The youngsters scuttle up to Sola the minute they see her. They know who Angel is but they don't know who this little girl is. Sola immediately hides herself behind mom's legs.

The adults slowly get off their feet and walk up to Angel and Sola to greet them warmly. The great pride showers Angel and Sola with affections. This is a big moment for Sola. Crossing the threshold from exclusive-mother-daughter relationship to seventeen-member-pride relationship overwhelms the little one. Nevertheless, she likes to be the center of attention and cherishes the fanfare. When mom nudges her, she comes out of mom's shield and enjoys the spot light.

Sola is especially attracted to Dave, a giant male lion with splendid-black mane. She *pitter-patter* trots towards Dave and nuzzles up to him. Gazing upon his tiny offspring he starts tenderly licking her and says, *"This is my child who carries my gene. To fulfill my role as a father I will lay down my life to defend you from aggressors."*

## The Ultimate Test

In July the rainy season is over, and the dry season sets in. Everywhere you look in the Ruana Plain you see parched ground and overgrazed land. It is the repeat of the familiar scene that occurs in this migration odyssey. Instinct of survival always kicks in when migrants are faced with such dilemma. After a few months when the grassy land is depleted to barren lands by two millions of grass-eaters, the mass moves on.

This time things have gotten worst. Under the blistering African sun waterholes are drying up. Faced with thirst and hunger, the mega-herd would be pushed to their very limits of endurance in the battle of staying alive.

Apart from lack of water and nourishment, animals suffer from heat strokes and diseases. Lots of them drop to ground while marching. These casualties aren't destined to complete the annual circle. However, in the mystery of life cycle, herbivores' losses are predators' gains. The phenomenon allows scavengers to feed on abundant carcasses.

In the zebra herd, Moses once more gallops up and down looking for a new piece of grassy land. This time, it's not going to be easy. He knows it. The Runana Plain is a much smaller plain than any other plain in the Serengeti. That is why after two months of grazing the mega-herd is forced to move on.

*"Ruth, I have searched every corner in the field without finding a decent piece of patch for grazing. I am afraid that we have to move on now to cross the Mara River."*

*"So be it. We got do what we got to do. Who wants to stay here waiting to die? I have seen animals dropping here and there. Staying here would mean to end like them,"* says Ruth in anguish, and she continues, *"We were lucky when we crossed the Grumetic River. Our family suffered no casualty. Maybe crossing Mara will be as*

*safe as crossing Grumetic.*" Her spirit is boosted with some positive thinking.

*"I hope so."*

The Mara River awaits the meg-herd with its swift current and steep bank. Moses remembers how each year animals would scramble for the same space of the steep muddy bank; their instinct of following each other would create a bottleneck, causing a mass built up behind. How chaotic! Astute Moses wants not to follow the crowd.

*"To avoid the frenzy, we are to divert the passageway. I know another crossing point not used by the mega-herd. The sweeping current has deterred the animals. But for us, daring and good swimmers, it's a challenge worth taking. Com'on, let's veer off to another crossing point. Fear not, my fellow zebra, we shall overcome and shall cross the daunting river,"* says Moses to his harem.

In the wildebeest and Tomson's gazelle's herds, a gauntlet of perils has likewise struck the animals for the past few weeks. The worst is yet to come. But to them, the same; if running for lives means to cross the Mara River, so be it. The mirage of green pastures on the other side of the river relentlessly drives them to push their limits.

The mega-herd is at the ultimate-test point in the struggle for staying alive. Before even reaching the Mara River, there will be days of stampeding under scorching hot sun without water and food. Once they reach the river bank, thirst will prompt them to linger along the shoreline to drink. There, danger is, again, lurking.

Hungry crocodiles are expecting their annual feast. The cunning killers are hiding in the muggy water, trying not to cause any ripple to arouse drinkers' suspicion. The veteran migrants know better and detect the swirling water pool and leap back just in time to escape crocodiles' attack. The inexperienced youngsters, unsuspicious of the apparent calm that masks a sinister threat, continue drinking. They are snatched off in a splash by the crocodiles' sudden attacks.

The horrific scene of the Grumetic River crossing replays at the Mara River. Blood oozes out into the flowing water. Screaming of desperate animals is everywhere. Fifty percent of youngsters born this year are separated from their mothers during the turmoil, but ninety percent of them are reunited on the other side of the river. Ten percent of them are either drown or eaten by crocodiles.

Surprisingly, the Serengeti's big cats aren't the main cause of death for the Serengeti's migration herd. As a matter of fact seventy-five percent of death is caused by drought, starvation, and drowning, disease. Only twenty-five percent of death is due to predation.

It is September. The migration moves into Kenya's Maasai Mara where fresh water is abundant and new grass has grown since the mega-herd's exodus last November. The circle is complete. The mega-herd animals will make themselves home here till grass runs out. To everyone's amazement, in spite of the heavy casualties the mega-herd suffered during the migration odyssey, two million wildebeest and zebra and gazelle have arrived. The same number as it was in the exodus. As a result of the balance of the ecosystem, the mega-herd population is kept intact.

Moses and his harem are home for now. When time comes, he will lead again in another round of migration odyssey with two rivers to cross.

# The Epilogue

Nature has its way in procreating life and maintaining balance. A look at the wilderness un-intervened by human ingenuity reveals the creative hands of a creator. It is inspiring to see how the creator designates *family* as the basic unit in the scheme of procreation, in the forming of a society for each species. Father and Mother each plays a role destined by nature.

After the family unit is formed (it maybe as small as mother and child), family bonding comes as a second nature. The family that stays together and supports one another is a viable family. The glue that unites them all is *love*. The phenomenon of love is evidenced no less in human family than in animal family, each according to its uncanny capability. Isn't this insight uplifting and inspirational for a searching soul?

Unfortunately, today the Serengeti Plain is faced with two perils: one, illegal poaching which has brought big cats close to extinction; the other, excessive lumbering which causes rivers to slowly dry up. If no action is taken to halt the impending demise, the Serengeti landscape will be history. We must pay attention to the well-being of wildlife if we want the wilderness adorned with more lovely scenes of mothers cradling cubs with tender care, the fun and game of sibling bonding. Don't we want a more beautiful and wonderful world to live in and the seventh New Wonder of the World to continue its stampeding? The good news is the dream is not far fetched. It is within our power to save the endangered big cats from extinction, to preserve a piece of Africa pristine in the wild. Then let's *do* it!

www.ingramcontent.com/pod-product-compliance
Lightning Source LLC
Chambersburg PA
CBHW060643290526
45793CB00001B/375